UNTRAPPED
FREEDOM MANIFESTO

UNTRAPPED
FREEDOM MANIFESTO

Become an Entrepreneur to Escape the Grind

and Find Freedom & Happiness

BRIAN CARRUTHERS

UNTRAPPED

Published by Pinnacle Press

Editing and layout by Paul Braoudakis

www.briancarruthers.com

ISBN: 978-1-7331906-0-2

Printed in the United States of America

PINNACLE PRESS

CONTENTS

It would be such an honor if you would write a review of this book on Amazon.

If you feel this book would benefit your friends, take a selfie with it and post it on social media. You will get serious likes and engagement ... and Thank You's!

It's our goal to get this book into as many hands as possible, because I know we can help so many people live better lives. To help make this happen, we created a bulk discount program to give you the ability to have plenty of copies on hand.

Give this book to anyone in your organization who needs a jolt to take their business to new heights.

Bulk pricing:

1-9	$12
10-24	$9
25-49	$8
50-99	$7
100-499	$6
500+	$5

Go to UntrappedBook.com

ACKNOWLEGMENTS

I have so much gratitude in my heart for so many people contributing to my life and to where I am today. To be able to write a book like this is only possible after having gone through the journey myself and having some incredible mentors, influences, and supporters.

I first want to express how blessed I am to have such a supportive wife, Melissa, who is the rudder to our lives for us and our three amazing boys – Talan, Colton, and Aiden. It is such a blessing to have a partner in life who encourages me to keep mentoring and contributing to others. This is quite selfless on her part, and in that way she is helping make other people's lives better.

I was raised by parents who embodied much of what I describe in this book. Not everyone is born into an entrepreneurial home, and because my parents chose that path, I had it woven into the fabric of my mindset. Much of my drive in life was always to make my parents proud, and even after they have expressed their pride, it's still the wind in my sails to this very day.

I was lucky enough to find myself in a business with billionaire Paul J. Meyer, known by many as the grandfather to the entire personal development industry. I learned more about wealth, freedom, contribution, service to others, and "passing it on" from him than anyone else. And the good news is that the basis of his philosophies came from the Bible and his associations with some of the world's biggest leadership influencers of the last 60 years. Paul, I miss you every day since you left us.

Back in 2012, I was asked by an early mentor in my life, Eric Worre, to come speak at an event for home-based business entrepreneurs. It was at that event that he encouraged me to think about how I could serve a greater audience and change more lives with my gifts. That was the day I decided to write my first book. Now here I am writing this, my fourth book, to continue my quest to help more people find freedom and happiness. Thank you, Eric, for enlarging my vision.

At age 24, I met a young man who I had no idea would have such an impact on my life. He has been a business partner with me for 21 years, we have spoken together on many stages to hundreds of thousands of people, he joined me at the altar at my wedding, and he is one of my greatest friends. Thank you, Darnell Self, for being so inspiring on this journey with me.

So here I am with four books, countless training courses, an active blog, and constant ideas popping into my head. All of this has been made possible because someone like Paul Braoudakis came into my life. This man deserves so much credit and he is certainly leaving his mark on the world via our works together. Gratitude for you fills my heart, Paul.

There are so many people in my life who inspire me, challenge me, cause me to grow, and who have been part of my journey thus far. You know who you are, and I appreciate the time we have spent together. I hope that I have added value to your life as well. And to those I have never met, maybe this will be the beginning of our connection. Cheers to your best future.

PROLOGUE

I sit on the couch in my master bedroom with my morning vitamin/protein smoothie. It's 10:15 a.m. on a serene Tuesday morning. I peer out the large picture window to my left, looking down over the 16th fairway and across the mighty Potomac River. This historic waterway flows more than 370 miles, from the Allegheny Mountains to the Chesapeake Bay and finally into the Atlantic Ocean. And along its path, it majestically cuts through the back of our development. My house is perched on top of a high bluff, affording me a spectacular view of the wildest river in the world. It's a view I never tire of.

It's a mostly sunny day, and everything seems so serene. My oldest son is in school and my wife is downstairs with our newborn and 20-month-old sons. Looking down upon the Potomac as it calmly flows past, I am overwhelmed by this feeling of exhilarating wonderment.

How did I get here? How is it that my life is this great?

You see, it wasn't always like this. In what seems like my "previous life," I would be off bright and early in the morning to the real estate office that employed me. I would sometimes work 12-hour days, coming home so tired that

I wouldn't want to talk to anyone. I was working 60 hours a week, putting endless miles on my car, and jumping every time a potential client called. That was my hectic life as a real estate agent. Don't misunderstand me; I enjoyed it. And I was making really good money for a young man in his 20's. In the thick of the grind, I didn't know there was anything better.

This is it, I thought. *This is the way to work hard and make a great living. If you want to have a good life, these are the sacrifices you make for it.*

I know what it's like to say "no" to friends who invited me to join them on a trip or come out for the evening. I know what it's like to have to put my career first, ahead of friendships and sometimes even family. I know what it's like to look at price tags and understand that nothing in life comes free and everything you want takes hard work. I watched my parents work hard to provide for us. It's what we do, and it's noble.

So ... how did I get *here*? As I'm perched on my couch looking out the window, the movie of my life is scrolling through my mind. I'm seeing myself as a youngster playing with my siblings and friends. That was a life without stress, without worry. Outside of school, I just went with the flow and focused on things I enjoyed.

Then I see my college years as kind of a blur. I didn't see myself using the degree I was going to come away with, so those years were mostly about the social experience for me. I pretty much knew I was going to follow in my father's footsteps and sell real estate in his company. Once home from college, I took my final summer to work at the beach before thrusting myself into my real estate career. For several years, that was my focus in life: to make Rookie of the Year for my home county, and to be making six figures by the age of 25. And guess what? I achieved both.

I was making more money than any of my friends. I bought my first house at 24. I was so proud of myself, and so much of that pride was in knowing that my parents were proud of me. I was a hard worker.

Then that fateful day came when I met some entrepreneurs who changed my life. My mind expanded and could never go back to its original form. I saw a bigger life, a better, more fulfilling life. How could this be? I was making good money, my parents were proud, and my friends respected my success. What more was there?

My eyes opened to a new world of possibilities. Could it be for real that you could make far more money while enjoying true time freedom? You mean I could ditch the grind of an over-stuffed calendar, wouldn't have to jump when someone called, wouldn't have to report in to an office daily, and could make six figures a month rather than per year? I will never forget the day when these entrepreneurs shared the details of their lifestyles. I was in a state of utter disbelief. How could there be a better path than the one I was already on?

That thought still sticks in my head as I gaze out the window.

That first house I was living in back when I was 24 was a 2,200-square-foot home in Maryland. It was older and needed a bit of work. Now I'm sitting in this 8,000-square-foot palatial home with literally a million-dollar view. My Ford Explorer has been replaced by a Ferrari, a Bentley GT convertible, a Lincoln Navigator, and my wife's Audi Q7. I have many investment properties, large investments in stocks, bonds, private equity funds, and I even bought the northern tip of North Caicos in the Turks and Caicos Islands. I have total time freedom, which dawns on me as I sit on this couch on a Tuesday morning sipping my smoothie while most of the world is smack dab in the middle of the hustle and bustle of their perfunctory workday.

Please understand that I don't list my "things" or assets for the purpose of bragging. Rather, they are part of my freedom story, and to overlook them would be a slap in the face of gratitude. I am blessed beyond words and profoundly grateful! I am humbled that something this great can be real for my family. But I also feel like there is something more. If my life is this good, I have this deep yearning to help others to have a similar reality. I want them to feel this same surreal peace of mind and sense of accomplishment.

In one way, I feel like I have arrived, but in another very real way, I haven't arrived at all until I've helped every other person out there who dreams about a similar destiny for themselves and their families. Now that I've made the entrepreneurial shift and created this dream-like reality, I have this insatiable desire — more like a mission — to spread the word and show others the way. After all, someone showed me the way. I would have never figured this out on my own. I would still be stuck in the old grind, not knowing that better was possible. I would have swallowed the proverbial blue pill (no, not *that* one! The one from the movie *The Matrix*!) and lived in blissful ignorance of a more powerful and liberating reality.

I have found the way to create a life where I can have fun, help people, and make a fortune all at the same time. This was not a possibility on the path I was previously on. Learning the ins and outs of becoming an entrepreneur has radically altered the course of my life and has reshaped my destiny in positive ways I never dreamed possible. For this reason, I feel a sense of moral obligation to share it with the world.

My assumption is that the reader is likely an employee working for someone else. Or maybe you own a business, but perhaps not the kind that will deliver financial and time freedom simultaneously. I don't want to come across as believing that having a job is a bad thing. There are many important jobs out there that someone needs to do in order for the world to keep spinning. There is an endless supply of people in the world who will surely fill that demand in those roles. But you don't have to be one of them. If you would rather take your life to a whole new level that you either never knew about or never thought was possible for you, I'm here to tell you that there is a way. My hope is that this book will open your mind to a whole world that you may not have thought was available to you.

It is, and it's there for the taking. And if you're coachable and teachable, I'll help you get there.

INTRODUCTION

If you're reading this book, chances are you don't want to be stuck in your same job when you're 60 years old (unless, of course, you're already at that age. Take heart; there's hope for you as well!). Frankly, you might not want to be stuck there a year from now. It is my goal to help you go from just *dreaming* the dream to *living* the dream. I have spent the last several years of my life showing people how I found my way off the proverbial treadmill, created wealth and freedom, and now live a life on my own terms filled with purpose and contribution ... *so that they can do it, too.*

That last line is most important, otherwise this book would be nothing more than a bragging manifesto. Plenty of other people have also done it, and there's no shortage of them willing to toot their own horns to tell you about it! But they won't tell you *why* they did it, much less *how*. They just want you to know they made it. This book is not about them or me. It's about you.

Much of this book is focused on my goal of *convincing you* to see my point of view on why your life will become 10 times happier once you become an entrepreneur. That is the

One third of all Americans have not saved any money for retirement.

Source: GoBankingRates.com

absolute priority. If you aren't convinced *why to*, then the rest of the *how to* ideas won't make any difference at all. My goal here is to start with *Why* and then introduce a few *Hows*. If this book can help you merely solidify the *why* in your mind, I will be proud to know that I helped change someone's life.

Let me also state from the beginning that being "trapped" has nothing to do with your income level. Yes, the mid-level manager earning $62,000-a-year and working 60-plus hours a week is trapped. The $34,000-a-year factory worker who has faithfully punched in every single day for the last 30 years is trapped. But I know people who are making $500,000 a year who are trapped. Being trapped is more than income; it's a mindset that requires a radical shift.

Because I've already made the successful shift myself and succeeded in becoming a wealthy entrepreneur, I know 100% that this is the path to freedom and happiness for you. I am sold, and there is nothing you can tell me that could convince me otherwise. So don't bother trying. Don't tell me you're already as happy and free as you want to be. I won't buy it, so save your breath.

As you take this journey with me, you are going to have some epiphanies. We can do it the hard way where you try to argue counterpoints against each idea, or you can read this book with a more open-minded approach and *look for reasons you can agree with me*. The latter approach is best because all I am trying to do is help you take your life to a new level. It's not for my gain but for yours.

You may not feel like you're trapped right now, because you are living a life that you're used to. But once you read this book and realize that your life is good but great is possible, you'll have a new frame of reference. Maybe you've convinced yourself that things are "good." But as leadership expert Jim Collins reminds us, "good" is the enemy of "great." The distance between good and great is measured not in inches but in *miles*. Sometimes in light years.

I'm here to tell you that *great* is not only possible, it's well within your reach.

I wish I could say that this book is going to create a revolution of millions of people who become entrepreneurs and get untrapped from the rat race. But that's already been happening. I speak to 10,000-person audiences at a time on this subject. I've shared stages with Richard Branson, Tony Robbins, Grant Cardone, Eric Worre, Pitbull, Jack Canfield, Daymond John, and Robert Kiyosaki. We are all champions of the free enterprise system that allows anyone willing to harness their dreams and commit to a journey of consistent, solid work ethic to build their own empire.

So if you decide to go for it, rest assured you won't be the first. You will be no guinea pig testing something on yourself. You will be testing something *in* yourself — do you have the guts to rise above the crowd you are surrounded by and reach for something greater?

This book just may be what you needed to read in order to muster up the confidence to rally around good reasons to join the many success stories that have blazed the trail before you.

Join the revolution so you can revolutionize your own life.

UNTRAPPED

Have you ever felt trapped in a life that was not the one you pictured when you were younger and dreaming of your future? Give this a go and see if it resonates with you at all.

You grew up watching your parents work hard. They conditioned you to believe that the way to make it in life was to go to school, get a degree, get a good job, and work hard every day to make an honest living. Make sacrifices, make more good choices than bad, and give up this for that. Maybe you saw them give up time with you so they could work lots of hours to make money to provide for the family. Or maybe they chose to put more value on family time and therefore sacrificed a bigger income and a lifestyle with more options and luxuries. Either way, you saw firsthand that life is sometimes a series of tradeoffs.

So, here you are in *your* life. Here is the ultimate question:

Is *this* how you thought you'd be living at this point in your life?

By 2033, Social Security will need to be cut by 23%

Source: Social Security Administration

It is absolutely critical that you stop and really ponder that question. Be honest. Brutally.

Is *this* how you thought you'd be living at this point in your life? You've been at your job for how long? How far along are you towards "living the dream?"

I am starting this book off with so many questions because that is how you find answers. Most people don't know how to ask the right questions. If you don't discover *why* you should change your life for the better, you certainly won't spend a moment learning *how* to do it. Always start with *why* if you want to find meaningful answers.

So please allow me to run you through another line of questioning. I want to help you learn how to question things. Life never has to remain the way it is, unless you choose to let life simply happen to you.

Is this the life you *want* to be living? I know you're living it, but is it what you *want*? Let me be clear, I am not asking if you are happy with your present life. The reason I won't bother is that many people convince themselves to be happy with what they've got. They really want to be doing something more, but they settle. They find a way to be content with it.

Just the word "settle" makes my stomach turn. How would you feel if you overheard your spouse telling someone he/she "settled" in deciding to marry you, and that you aren't what he/she really dreamed of? Could you live with that? I bet it would devastate you.

What if you review your life from the outside looking in, and ask yourself, "Did I settle?" Maybe you had dreams of career, travel, fun, family, contribution, impact, and meaning. But your current reality is not what you pictured your life to be. Maybe you're in a job that has little to do with your childhood dreams. Maybe you are not even using the degree you invested so much to acquire. Maybe you have a demanding boss who makes you feel unappreciated or underpaid. Maybe you feel your advancement opportunities are limited.

Or maybe you're doing really well at the top of your game, making a huge income and you have the respect of people all around you — but there's something missing. Maybe you feel like you aren't leading a purpose-driven life and you long for more meaning. You might be trapped living check to check, whether it's in the form of a salary or even big commissions. Or you might be trapped in a high paying job that you feel you can't let go of because the money is too good and you're addicted to the money fix. I imagine you feel trapped in at least one of these boxes, and certainly that's not a good feeling.

WHAT DO YOU WANT TO DO WITH YOUR LIFE?

There was a popular music video in the '80s that featured a militaristic father who despised his son's music. The young boy would lock himself in his room after school every day, strap on a guitar, play his favorite band's record, and lose himself in the fantasy of becoming like his rock 'n' roll heroes one day. The father suddenly bursts into the boy's room and berates him up and down for his taste in music, hobbies, clothes, and for daring to dream anything beyond his current reality.

Sixty percent of retirees don't budget for entertainment and activities.

Source: Merrill Lynch

Finally, the father gets within inches of the boy's face and, with veins popping out of his neck, yells to his son at the top of his lungs:

"What do you want to do with your life?!"

The boy pauses momentarily, and defiantly looks his father in the eye and boldly says, "I wanna rock!"

I love the tenacity and temerity of that young boy. He had a dream, a clear vision, and a steely determination to not let anyone — even his staff sergeant father — talk down his young and idealistic aspirations. His reply was crisp and to the point:

I wanna rock!

How about you? Do you wanna rock? What *do* you want to do? This is your chance to go back to the sandbox or the playground at 8 years old. What did you dream about doing when you grew up? What adventures and travels? What would you be getting awards for? How did you expect it would feel to be a grownup, calling your own shots, living how you want to live?

At the age of 8, did you dream about doing what you're doing right now? If so, did you think it would be far more fulfilling? Or maybe the career you ended up in is way far off from what you dreamed of as a kid. I know how this goes.

When you're 8, you can do or be anything your heart can dream up. A veterinarian, a firefighter, a flight attendant, a professional athlete, and, yes, even a rock star. But then you get into high school and your dream circle starts to shrink. You've got to think about college and what you'll study. Once you pick a major, your dream circle shrinks even more. Then you get out into the working world with that degree and you find such limited opportunities to use it. Your dream circle basically vanishes.

So you find the best option you can, and you embark down that path. In short, you settle. Maybe you're still on that path. Or maybe you couldn't find fulfillment there, and you've already moved on to a different path since then. Or maybe you've made even more directional shifts since then. You are searching for a life of happiness and fulfillment, so I commend you for having the courage to make moves in pursuit of better.

Are you bored?

Find yourself not happy?

Not excited about your life?

BE LIKE MIKE?

Let me ask you another crucial question: If you're the Michael Jordan of your job — nobody does your job better than you — and you bust your tail working that job better than anybody, will you ever be able to retire with your dream lifestyle in 20 years? Will you have all the time you want, and all the money you can spend? If the answer is "no," if you say, "My job does not offer that," then why keep going down that same path with no light at the end of the tunnel? The very definition of insanity ought to stop you dead in your tracks!

Unfortunately, most people are trapped in that very predicament. Maybe they never even ask themselves, "Will my job ever deliver what *I really want*?" They just kind of get into a rhythm and keep on going through the motions of life, but they never really stop and think, "My job's never going to give me what I want." If that's the case, if your job does not even have the possibility of giving you the lifestyle that you want, then you have to make a decision to do something different. *Something* has to change! If a lack of money is limiting your options, that has to change. Maybe you have money, but you've got no time — then *that* has to change. This is why I believe you need to become an entrepreneur.

I've never met a person who had a joyful, whole-hearted life but was miserable at work. We spend half our lives at work. That stuff will eat you alive. You bring the stress home and it infects your marriage, relationships with your kids and friends, and anything else you are trying to enjoy.

If you feel trapped, it's a 24-hour thing. It even affects your sleep time. We can't dismiss the stress and try to offset it by just shutting it out and having more fun in our downtime. It doesn't work. Your subconscious self is still stewing on it even when you are not consciously aware. This is why we all must seek joy in what we do for a living. Sure, nothing will ever be 100% constantly joyful, but it can be a majority of the time. It *can* be and *needs* to be. You cannot allow it to remain any other way.

Here is something I've learned over and over. *Having plenty of money and no time is no good, and having plenty of time but not enough money is no good.*

Having a happy balance of both time *and* money is what enables you to be happy and free, and allows you to design your life for maximum fulfillment and contribution. But let's be honest; having both at the same time is rare. Once you are free — meaning you have time *and* financial freedom — you can then experience the closest thing in life to true nirvana: having fun, helping others, and leaving your mark on the world. But is it even possible for you? Absolutely!

My favorite author and business coach of all time, Jim Rohn, always said, "You work hard all day at your job to earn a living, but you should be working spare time, nights or weekends, building your fortune." You may be working hard all day at your job to earn a living working for someone else and helping build *their* fortune, but are you doing something on the side to build *your* fortune for you and for your family?

It is important that you design your life with the end game in mind. If your job doesn't even offer the opportunity or the chance to achieve what you ultimately want for your life, there's no other choice. You've got to make a change. You've got to make a decision to become an entrepreneur.

WHY YOU NEED MORE MONEY

Let me paint a picture for you. One day you're going to want to retire. Maybe you've been a good person and you've got somebody to retire with. Maybe you have a spouse, so there's going to be two of you. At what age do you plan on retiring? Since the retirement age for most Americans is 65, let's go with that. Let's also assume that with good medicine and decent health you live 20 more years to 85.

So picture this. There are two of you. You want to eat three meals a day, right? So there are two people eating three meals a day, and let's say you're only going to spend $7 per meal. You're not going out and eating at nice restaurants. We are talking just $7 a meal. How many days a year do you want to eat? I'm going to go out on a limb and assume the answer is 365. So, two people eating three $7 meals a day, 365 days a year, for 20 years.

Do the math.

Do you realize that means you will to need to have $306,600 in the bank in order for you to simply be able to eat three $7 meals a day when you retire?

Let that sink in for a minute. That's $300,000 just to be able to eat three $7 meals! That does not include Christmas presents for the grandkids, going out to movies, your monthly utility bills, or going on a vacation. It's just to eat three $7 meals a day.

43% of Americans spend more than they receive each month then borrow and use credit cards to finance the shortfall.

Source: Federal Reserve

Now look at your bank account. How far are you from having $306,600 ready for your retirement? Most people, unfortunately, don't even have $10,000 to their name, much less $300,000. How much have you saved up at that job you've been working at for however many years? Are you ready for retirement? Next year? Ten years from now?

If you keep doing what you're doing, you're going to keep getting what you're getting. If you have not saved up a lot by now, how is that ever going to change? *That's* why you've got to make a decision to do something different. If you want to maintain a decent standard of life when you retire, you'll realistically need funds well into the millions.

Don't let that daunt you. Let it inspire you! Let it motivate you! Let it drive you to an exhilarating new future for you and your family!

I take pride in that I have always sought out wisdom from people I feel I can grow from (more on that in the chapter "The Key to Success"). I learned years ago that if someone else is living a lifestyle that I would love to live, I need to put my ego aside, ask good questions, then shut up and listen.

So one day I sat in a coffee shop with a very smart man. He had built himself an empire and was a very happy person. He seemed to have figured some key things out about life.

"Take out your checkbook and write me a check for the largest amount you could without it bouncing," he said casually. "What's that number?"

I sheepishly followed his directions and wrote a check as confidently and truthfully as I could. I slid it across the table toward him. He studied the number I had written down and then slowly looked up at me.

"You've been working at your career for *how* many years now? And *that's* the number you've got? How does that number make you feel?"

Gulp.

Sometimes we need a checkup from the neck up. I was so full of myself for making such a great income in real estate. Six figures, baby! But what I realized that day is how *much* income we make is irrelevant. What matters most is how much you've got at the end of the day — at the end of the year. If you're just churning and burning, making money to service debt and pay bills, and you're not building real wealth, then you're just spinning your wheels and not getting anywhere. The question my wealthy friend asked me was my wakeup call, and I am so glad I was humble enough to allow him to ask the questions I needed to hear. That very

Millennials who have student loans have $325,000 less in retirement savings than their debt-free peers.

Source: LIMRA

well might not have happened if my ego had gotten in the way.

The advice I took from my significant mentors is what I will pass along to you: Always be humble, drop your ego, choose the right people to learn from, and be an absolute sponge.

A big ego equals a small bank account. You've never learned enough. To this day, I still seek people playing at even higher levels than me and making a maximum impact. I'm a sponge any time I can get around these folks. I have so much more growing and *doing* in my future — and so do you!

GETTING FROM HERE TO THERE

You see people who are living the good life — maybe not someone you know personally, but you know they are out there. You read about them or you see them on TV. How did they get it all? They are living the lifestyle we all would love to live, calling their own shots and spending their time how they choose with whomever they choose. Their lives are making a difference in the world and serving others.

Can you imagine *yourself* living that kind of life? Maybe you stopped dreaming long ago, and you've conditioned yourself not to think like that in order to protect yourself from feeling defeated or unhappy. Again, maybe you have convinced yourself to be happy with the life you've got so that you don't see yourself as trapped in a life that is less than the one of your dreams.

I am here to tell you I have witnessed many people who had settled, but had their eyes opened to bigger possibilities and found the belief that they could live a better life — and this *belief* led them to take action. Today, they are living lives of real freedom and fulfillment. *They became untrapped in their minds, which unlocked the door for them to find the path to a better life.*

You want more, you want happier, you want it all. Don't let anyone ever tell you not to want it all! You're tired of the constant sacrifices, tired of playing small, tired of feeling like you're on a treadmill to oblivion going nowhere fast. You're sick and tired of being sick and tired. You don't want to just continue playing the hand you've been dealt. And upon reading these last few paragraphs, you are open to hearing about possibilities. You admit that you have settled somewhat and that deep inside yourself, you long for more and better. You may be ready to discard that hand and draw some new cards. But how?

It begins with *knowing*. Once you *know that you know* that you deserve better, and once you *know* that if others have done it you can too, that is the genesis of getting yourself from here to there. You *know* it's possible, because others have already done it. You must *conceive* in your own mind that your dream lifestyle of wealth, abundance, freedom and contribution is waiting for you.

STOP: Picture that life in your mind's eye right now.

DO NOT READ ON UNTIL YOU HAVE PAUSED AND PICTURED IT.

Next you must *believe*. Just because others have done it, doesn't automatically mean you believe *you* can. And just because you think you can, that doesn't mean you *know* you can. So you are going to have to be convinced that you've got what it takes, and *believe* in yourself that you can succeed doing something different than just being the pawn in someone else's game as an employee.

Let me make this very clear. I am not against working as an employee for someone else. Jobs are not bad. The alternative to not having a job for many people would mean no roof over their family's head, no food on the table, no clothes on their backs. Having a job is better than being unemployed and broke. What I'm advocating is that you don't have to settle for being trapped in the matrix of trading your time for money so that you can merely subsist and exist.

Maybe you love your job. You really enjoy what you do. You love your boss, your company, your role, your hours, your commute, your office, your coworkers, your salary, and your growth opportunities there. OK, you are that rare bird! It's amazing if you love all of that. But I am here to tell you that you can still benefit by becoming an entrepreneur on the side, and finding even more abundance and opportunities. In life, we are all either growing or we are dying. We experience life more fully when we are stretching and reaching for a higher potential.

And speaking of your job, you're going to need it for now, regardless. Why? Because making the shift to becoming an entrepreneur is not done in one night, but is more safely accomplished as a parallel pursuit with your career *until it can one day replace your job*. We will discuss this in the next chapter, "The Power of Part-Time."

ENTREPRENEURS HAVE ALL THE FUN!

Who are these people you always see and hear about who are taking exotic vacations every other month?

Hint: It's not employees.

Who are the people celebrating their wins as something personal?

Hint: It's not employees.

Who do you see buying new cars every few years?

Hint: It's not employees.

Who do you see volunteering all the time in support of great causes, and going on several mission trips each year?

Hint: It's not employees.

Who do you see golfing, fishing, or shopping at 11 a.m. on a random Monday?

Hint: It's not employees.

Only when you're your own boss, as an entrepreneur, can you do all the fun stuff.

Become an entrepreneur right away.

WHO IS MEANT TO BE AN ENTREPRENEUR?

You are.

I don't want to offer a huge history lesson here, but I need to point out that it is only in recent times that so many people began working for other people. Just a little over a century ago, many people were entrepreneurs, meaning they mastered a craft and sold that value to the marketplace. They were farmers, blacksmiths, tailors, carpenters, doctors, etc. They didn't seek employment; they worked for themselves.

Then along came the Industrial Revolution. Machinery made certain businesses scalable to accomplish more, and those business owners hired people to help them grow.

This began to further create social classes. The business owners became the upper class, and those who worked for them (depending on their jobs) became the middle and lower class.

The more recent Information Age has allowed for the rich to get richer for sure, but it has also opened the door to the rest of society to have the best chance to ascend into the upper class. There are so many opportunities now for anyone with courage, grit, and perseverance to rise up and seize any level of success they want. We know this by picking up any issue of *Fortune* or *Forbes* magazine, with the endless rags to riches stories. I get so inspired each and every time I read about how a person had an idea, birthed it from their garage or basement office, grinded it out for several years while barely holding on, and are now new entrants onto the prestigious *Forbes* Billionaires list.

Or even more common, the home-based entrepreneur who we may never hear about in a magazine. This person started a side business and built it on the side while working their job, and after a year or two they were able to replace their full-time income, fire their boss, and work 100% for themselves with full control of their time schedule.

You see, I am not here to define what success looks like for you. Maybe it's millions or billions, or maybe it's the same money you're used to making, but you just want to do it in your own business rather than building someone else's so that you get to call the shots. There is just something so magical about waking up in the morning knowing that any time/energy you put into your own business is building *your* dreams — building *your* empire.

THE CHOICE OF BEING A MOM OR DAD VS. HAVING A CAREER

There has always been a major life decision that a parent has to make when it comes to career vs. babies. Decades ago, it was rather customary that when a couple wanted to start a family the father would have a career to make a living, and the mother would stay home and raise the family. But times have changed and people's thinking around this has evolved. Families and homes are starting to look like the "nuclear family" less and less. Sometimes a dad stays home and the mom has the career. Sometimes both partners want to have careers that they are passionate about. A couple must decide how to best design their life as a family. There are also increasing numbers of single parents where there is no secondary choice, and those single parents have to earn a living while raising their children at the same time.

The good news is that moms and dads can have their cake and eat it, too! They can be full-time present parents, while at the same time have businesses of their own that they build around their life from home. So that fabled sacrifice of giving up on having a career in order to have kids is a relic

More than 3 billion adults worldwide don't understand basic financial concepts.

Source: Standard & Poor's

of the past. If there's *anything* they have to give up, it might be that one-hour commute to and from an office every day, being stuck at a job away from their kids for eight hours a day, having a boss dictate their schedule!

For those who would rather not live that life anyway, the home-based entrepreneur explosion has freed up many thousands of moms and dads who are now making great money from home while their main focus gets to be on their families. It has been so heartening to watch this shift over the last 20 years. I have watched hundreds of people I've personally worked with be able to retire from their jobs and work for themselves full-time from home. They get to be at all the kids' sporting events and recitals, do homework with them after school, have family meals, and just be present. They block time during the day to build their businesses, but with far more control than they ever would have had if they had jobs or traditional businesses.

This is the biggest reason I am a fan of home-based businesses that are turnkey and efficient. Whether you are a parent like me, or a single person, we all become happier when we have control over our schedules and can live our lives by our own design.

This doesn't have to be for *other* people; this can be you!

THE POWER OF PART-TIME

Once again, I must repeat one of the biggest life lessons I learned from my favorite business coach, Jim Rohn. He always said, "You work hard all day in your job to earn a living, but you should be working spare time nights or weekends building your fortune."

I know you, like everybody else, probably work very hard doing what you do at your job. You do it hard, you do it well, you put in the hours, and you bring home that paycheck. But at the end of the day, Rohn says that's not building your brand, it's not building your business, it's not building your fortune, and it's not building your retirement. You're trading your time for money with your employer. I love how he finishes his famous mantra: " … but it won't be long before I'm working *full-time* on my fortune."

So if your full-time job has not made you financially free yet, will it ever? How much money are you saving and investing every month right now? Do you have an actual plan to build your wealth? Most people spend more time planning a one-week vacation than they do planning their lives.

So let's talk about creating your plan. What's required? I

Half of American households currently live paycheck to paycheck.

Source: MarketWatch

believe it's a moment of disgust. One day you're going to wake up and you're going to say, "You know what? I'm sick and tired of being sick and tired. I want more from my life. I'm tired of not having time with my family. I'm tired of not being able to take the vacation I want to take. I'm tired of giving all of my most valuable hours to a job that doesn't really care about me."

When that moment of disgust hits you — I mean *really* hits you — the giant in you will awaken and the "why" for starting your own business will suddenly kick in. Your "why" will help you figure out the "how."

INVEST IN YOU

Let's not talk pie-in-the-sky. Let's talk real, and let's talk conservative. Let me show you some numbers that I think are going to blow your mind, that show how little you need to do to have a massive impact on your life. Take a look at the chart on the next page.

	10 years	20 years	30 years	40 years
$5 day ($150/month)	$30,982	$114,854	$341,898	$956,517
$10 day ($300/month)	$61,965	$229,709	$683,797	$1,913,034
$20 day ($600/month)	$123,931	$459,418	$1,367,595	$3,826,068
$50 day ($1,500/month)	$309,828	$1,148,545	$3,418,987	$9,565,170
$100 day ($3,000/month)	$619,656	$2,297,090	$6,837,975	$19,130,340

You can start a part-time business on the side that generates only an extra $600 a month, and then rather than spending that money you'll invest it. This is the key: *Don't spend the money!* It wasn't there before and you were still getting by without it. Pretend it's not there now, and put it to work *for* you!

If you did so at just a 10 percent annual return, compounded over time, do you know what that will mean to you? Well, $600 a month compounded over the next 10 years will generate $124,000 in your bank account. In 20 years, it'll grow to $459,000. In 30 years, it will grow to an astounding $1.3 million, and in just 10 more years, because of the magic of compounding, it will triple to a mind-blowing $3.8 million!

So as you look at your life and you're trying to decide what you want it to look like 10, 20, 30 years from now, at some point you'll probably want to retire. How much money are you going to need to retire? Do you need to have a million, $2 million, or $4 million? If you had $600 a month from a side business, you can see a plan right in front of you now. But what if you actually created a business that generated just an extra $1,500 a month?

Again, these are realistic numbers. I'm not talking about pie-in-the-sky getting rich overnight. If you made and invested an extra $1,500 a month compounded at 10 percent each year, that's $309,000. In 20 years, it's $1.1 million. In 30 years, it's $3.4 million, and in 40 years, it's more than $9 million dollars.

Over the last 40 years, the S&P Stock Index has averaged more than a 10 percent annual return. So when you think about that, I can predict that I can start a business part-time, a few hours a week. We call it slivers of time — 10 minutes here, 20 minutes there — building a part-time business generating an extra $600 a month. What might an extra $600 mean to you? How about an extra $1,500 a month? I'm going to go ahead and assume that the chart I just showed you got your wheels turning. I bet you're probably pretty excited about this.

Let go of *good* to grab *great*!

Will it be easy? Of course not.

Will it be worth it? Absolutely.

Life is hard. To continue to grind or struggle is hard. To build your success — that's hard, too. Choose your hard. I would pick the hard that has light at the end of the tunnel so that one day in the future the hard is gone and you can now live easier.

What's your dream? *How badly do you want it?*

Let's just stop for a moment, and do some make-believe. Pretend you suddenly had $50,000 a month of passive income coming in to you, guaranteed for life. What would you change in your life? What would you *stop* doing? What would you *start* doing?

STOP: CLOSE YOUR EYES FOR A FEW MINUTES AND ACTUALLY LET THIS PLAY OUT.

When I have done this exercise with thousands of people I've coached over the years, it was inspiring to hear the amazing dreams people had inside them, but sad at the same time because most of them had given up on any hope that those dreams would ever see the light of day. Some were artists but never had the time to let it out. Some wanted to go volunteer in third-world countries but didn't have the means to leave their job to do it. Some just wanted a nicer house in a decent neighborhood to raise their family, and others simply wanted to be debt free and not be working every waking hour so they could truly enjoy family time. Some had an idea for an invention and just didn't have the resources to turn it into reality.

The cemeteries, as they say, are filled with books that have never been written, works of art that have never been completed, and dreams that have never been fulfilled. So sad.

Of all the successful entrepreneurs I have come to know and call my friends, I cannot even begin to tell you all of the incredible stories of dreams that did come true. There are simply too many. I watched people who, once upon a time, were trapped in a life as an employee with limited time and money, but are now living the dream.

Jordan always wanted to learn to fly a helicopter, and he recently bought his own, which he flies often.

Darnell always wanted to spread his faith and help those in need, and he's now adopted villages in Haiti and the Dominican Republic.

Steve went to Yankees games as much as he could when he was living check to check, but recently took an entire year and traveled to *all* 162 Yankee games — and set a world record to boot! He liked it so much he fulfilled another dream to write a fantastic book — *162* — about the experience.

Kim grew up with limited means and appreciated kids who didn't have good family environments. So she now spends half the year giving her time to the orphanages she's built in Guatemala.

In the chapter "In Their Own Words" toward the back of this book, you'll hear from other real-life entrepreneurs who also took the risk and changed their lives forever.

Again, what are your dreams? What do you *really* want?

It's not a lack of resources that holds people back, it's a lack of *resourcefulness*. If you want your dreams badly enough, you find a way. Don't listen to everyone else who had dreams they've buried in the dirt because they stopped trying to figure out a solution. They have been conditioned and programmed for most of their lives to believe that you have to get a job, and it takes priority over anything else because you "have to make a living and pay your bills." Pay bills? Not one person ever dreams about paying bills! When you make the shift to becoming an entrepreneur and you find the vehicle to allow you to get money as an issue out of the way in your life … *now* you get to start digging up those dreams you buried long ago in your back yard.

THE TRIFECTA OF SUCCESS

Other than eating and sleeping, everyone spends their time doing three things — having fun, working for money, or helping people. Wouldn't it be amazing if you found a career or business that enabled you to do all three at one time?

The holy grail would be to do all of these things simultaneously because what you chose to do for a living not only pays extremely well, but you love doing it and you are helping people in the process. Is this possible to find? Yes — I found it. So have many others. You may even find yourself one day feeling the way I do — I feel I found my "calling."

Is what you're doing right now your "calling?" Does it call to you when you're on vacation and have you itching for vacation to be over because you can't wait to get back to it? If not, you haven't found your calling. I enjoy holidays, but I also can't wait for them to be over because I'm itching to reengage!

WHY YOU NEED TO BECOME WEALTHY

Money makes the world go 'round. You know it. I know it. We can either become the master of money, or be a slave to it for our entire lives. When someone tells me, "money can't buy you happiness," I ask them, "So you're saying being *broke* will buy you happiness?" Having a lot of money does not guarantee you'll be happy. I know plenty of rich people who aren't happy. Some lead admittedly miserable lives. If you have no sense of meaning in your life or connection with others, having a big bank account will do you no good. In fact, it could even isolate you from finding happiness. On the other hand, if your life has purpose and connection, and you have an abundance of money that allows you to fund doing things that matter to you, this is how you'll find optimal joy.

I'm not talking about being "rich," which is an adjective of a certain standard of living high on the hog. I am not saying that you should be motivated to pursue owning $1,000 handbags or $10,000 wristwatches. You may not even care to drive the nicest luxury car, own a mansion, or float around on a yacht. But *if* you do, that doesn't make you a bad person! Nice things are nice, and if you figure out the money game and can afford them, more power to you. But again, I want delve into something much different than being rich. I feel it is your duty, your responsibility to yourself and those you love, to build your wealth.

Wealth is a noun, and in many regards it's also a measurement of time. It represents how long your lifestyle would last if your source of income went away. For example, if your cost of living was $5,000 a month, and you have $100,000 to your name, what if you lost your job or source of income tomorrow? How long would your money last before you ran out and found yourself losing your home and you were out on the street? In this example, that answer would be 20 months. Would you feel "wealthy?" Not likely.

Now if you had $1 million put away and this happened, you would have 200 months (just over 16 years) before you would run out. I bet you'd feel a bit more secure, right? But even in this case, what if you outlived those 16 years and you had to go back to work?

The average financial planner estimates that to retire with a moderate lifestyle, and live that way for 20 years after retirement, one would need about $2.8 million to be put away. How close are you to that number? Do you have a plan to get there or beyond? Does your plan have you working your whole life away (your best years that you can never get back) just trying to save up enough money to start living when you're old? That's hardly a good life plan.

I believe you can design a roadmap to create the kind of income necessary to allow you to live well *now* and *later*. This is why I have to convince you to get focused on building your wealth immediately.

Maybe you are working each and every day right now earning a living and paying your bills. Some people aren't even doing well enough to get all of their bills paid each month. So if you are in the green and have money left over each month, you are at least not under water. But I will explain why you are still falling behind. It's due to what I call "servicing debt" versus "building wealth," which I go into extensively in my book *Money Mindset*.

Using the same example of your bills being $5,000 a month, let's say your income is $6,000 a month. Most people make the $6,000, pay the $5,000, and blow the leftover $1,000. Why? Because it was "extra." Their bills were paid, and that was always what mattered.

"As long as my bills are paid, I'm happy!"

Oh, what a horrible mindset! That kind of thinking will lead you to living in fear, check to check, praying to never lose your job or income, fearing disaster will fall upon your life. And you will never be able to stop working. Ever.

Instead, using a wealth-building mindset, what if your goal from day one in the month was to *build wealth* and not to just pay your bills? In this case, you made $6,000, you paid the $5,000 in debt/bills, and you don't treat the remaining $1,000 as "extra." That money is the only money you cared about, because it's the only money that belongs to you! You can put away some money every month into a wealth-building account, invest it, and have it growing and compounding every day. Do you realize that even small amounts added to this strategy every month can build such wealth that you can retire early as a millionaire?

Here is the main point: It's the *philosophy*. You can plug in any amount to this formula and see how much wealth you can amass. But the most important thing is a decision. You have to *decide* that building your wealth is important, and it must become urgent in your life. If you continue to service debt going forward like you have been up until now, then you are destined to keep living in scarcity and fear. Who wants to live like that? You would think *everyone* wants to — because a majority of the population does it! The truth is, they don't know any better. This stuff is not taught in schools. But you don't have to be a *slave* to money like the masses; you can learn to be the master of money like successful people.

Money cannot think or act; it is merely an instrument. You can learn how to acquire more money and use it to make your life better. You can also learn how to let your money grow itself and accelerate your wealth building. But here's a newsflash:

All money is not equal.

While no form of income is bad — I will take it all — some forms are far better than others. Once you get educated on the different forms of income, you can decide which ones you want to spend your time and energy pursuing. (And I bet it won't be the kind you're pursuing currently).

THREE FORMS OF INCOME

L ike I said, we won't turn away any money, as every dollar helps towards our goal of building wealth. But certain income is way better than others. I ask that you pay close attention here, as I am about to help you see how you can get yourself untrapped from the need for the grind.

Let's assume I have you semi-convinced that you need to do something new, that you need to start some kind of a side business to supplement your job that has the chance to give you the result you're looking for. The book I mentioned previously, *Money Mindset,* became a #1 best-seller in its category on Amazon very, very quickly when it first came out. Why? It's because money is a very important topic. A lot of couples fight about it. A lot of people are stressed about it. Most people don't know how to attract it. They don't know how to keep the money that they make. They don't know how to grow the money they make.

These are the three forms of income that you can create:

- **Linear income** - Only earning on what *you* do, trading your time for money as an employee or being self-employed.

- **Leveraged income** - Business owner with lots of people working for you who create revenue.

- **Residual income** - Do something once and keep getting paid forever. Get a customer once, repeatedly get paid.

Let's explore each income model ...

LINEAR INCOME

This is you trading your time for money. It's doing work and collecting a paycheck. I don't care if you are earning $10/hour working at McDonald's, $100/hour giving massages, $400/hour as an attorney billing hours, $10,000 per sale as a real estate agent, or $20,000 per surgery as a surgeon. If you don't work, you don't get paid. You are living check to check. If you stop working, your income stops. What if you get sick, can't work, want to retire, or lose your job? Your income disappears, and your life is upended. This is no way to live, in such fear. It's a grind that you're trapped in. It's you in a jail cell, running on a never-ending treadmill to oblivion.

The doctor who delivered my last two sons has been delivering babies for about 20 years. If a baby is to be born, he has to be there to do it. He's had to sacrifice and miss lots of precious times with his wife and his own kids to be at the hospital delivering someone else's. After factoring out all of his overhead, staff, malpractice insurance, etc., he's basically making a decent living. But he works long hours and he's always on call. Yet most people think being a doctor is a glamorous life. It's noble, it's amazing, but it is not working smart, getting ahead, or having time freedom to enjoy life while you're younger.

I know a real estate agent who was making $300,000 a year when the market was pretty hot. She was on fire and was designing her lifestyle based on this income having no end. But the market turned, and she had to suddenly work twice as hard to make about half the income. When you are the only source of income, and something outside of your control happens, this is scary.

I know a really great football player who made it to the NFL. But soon after, he blew out his knee and it ended his career. He had to scramble to figure what to do next to trade his time and talent for a paycheck. He has since bounced from career to career trying to find his path. His dreams were hitched to his talent alone, and his ability to perform himself. When that came to a halt, so did his earning power.

As you can tell, I am not a fan of linear income. That being said, I suppose linear income is good — out of GOOD, BETTER, BEST. So let's find out what's *better* and *best* ...

LEVERAGED INCOME

Leverage means you are not relying on earning from solely your own efforts, but rather overriding the efforts of lots of people. This is how most wealthy people got there. To have leveraged income is to incorporate the efforts of other people to generate your cash flow.

Would you rather be the real estate *agent* or the *broker*? The insurance *agent* or the *broker*? The agent gets paid only on the basis of their own efforts, but the broker gets paid on the transactions of *all* of his agents. The people who have people working for them make the most money and they tend to have the most time freedom.

I was very fortunate to be raised by my father who understood and taught me a business principle that most people go to their grave never figuring out. He said, "Brian, you can go out and sell houses and make a bunch of money. But, would you rather work *hard* or would you rather work *smart*? Wouldn't you rather be the real estate *broker* and have hundreds of agents out there working for you and get a little piece of action from each of their sales?" That was a light bulb moment for me.

J.Paul Getty, one of the first recorded billionaires in American history, once said, "I'd rather get paid 1% off the efforts of 100 people, than 100% off only my own efforts." Profound, right? In my opinion, if 100% of your income comes from 100% of your own efforts, you're setting yourself up for disaster. At best, you might squeak by in a mediocre lifestyle.

Let's say you had a business selling cell phones, and the profit margin was $100 per phone. Which scenario would you rather have?

a. You personally sell 20 a month and earn yourself $2,000.

b. You recruit a team of 100 salespeople who each sell 20, but you give them $80 and you keep $20. Two thousands sales times your $20 override is $40,000 to you!

In this example, you make more per sale on a linear income basis — $100 each! The leveraged income is only $20 each, but you aren't the one doing the work to earn it. This income is PASSIVE. And you get the scaling effect by earning off the sales of as many people as you want to hire! You'll have time freedom earning the $40,000 in passive override income, while if it was just you, you'd have to personally be grinding out those sales every month to still only make a fraction of the income. My advice: Don't be a grinder — a pawn in someone else's game — by giving *them* leveraged income and time freedom. Get this for *yourself*!

I have many friends who have businesses where they have built large sales teams selling all sorts of different products. Some sell health products, others sell beauty products, and others sell different services. These friends are enjoying leveraged income in big fashion, some earning six and even seven figures of passive income.

My very own dad showed me, by his own example, the power of leveraged income. He built a large 35-office real estate company when I was growing up. He made many millions of dollars because of the leveraged income from all those agents selling houses within his firm. Yes, they were selling houses for themselves, but he was benefitting greatly because he earned an override from each of them. My parents were wealthy, and I watched them do it. I am forever grateful for the great life they provided for us.

My mom was at home raising us kids, and was very hands-on in our lives. She also helped run the company and ran all their books. My dad worked his heart out growing the company. Frankly, it was the stress of building such a huge business with all of the exposure and risk of office leases, staff, payroll, market conditions, competition and so on, that resulted in his first heart attack by age 32.

Creating leveraged income is certainly important if you want to build wealth and provide for your family; just be careful to pick the right business and find one with low exposure to risk and stress. There are such businesses out there that I work with (more on that in a later chapter).

RESIDUAL INCOME

Are you ready for the "holy grail" form of income? Residual income is income that you receive over, and over, and over, and over, and over, for what you did *one time*. This is *the ultimate* income source, and frankly it is *the* most important concept in this entire book.

If you get nothing else from reading it, I hope you at least come away with the hell-bent mission of getting residual income into your life.

Once you know about residual income, if you have it you'll get what I mean. If you don't go get some, this will haunt you for the rest of your life. How will you ever put this concept out of your brain once you've discovered it?

Examples:

Michael Jackson is still one of the Top 100 highest-earning entertainers in America in 2019 (and he died in 2009). How? He recorded a song *one time*, but every time it plays, he (his estate, now) gets paid. That's residual income.

My insurance agent has insured all of my homes and cars for more than 20 years as of this writing. She signed up the policies one time, and they renew every year automatically without even having to call me. And she gets automatic renewal or residual income every time these renew, every year! Seriously, the only time we talk is when I'm adding another home or another car to my driveway. Yet she just keeps collecting those residuals. God bless her. Somebody had to write my policies, and collect those residuals.

Real estate investors plunk down big chunks of capital to purchase homes that can be rented out, thereby creating rental income. This is a form of residual income, but there's a catch. Not only does the investor need to find the money to put down to buy each home at a price where the rent will be higher than their monthly mortgage payment to create positive cash flow, but being a landlord is not fun. Trust me, I know — I own a number of properties. Regular maintenance is not only a pain to keep up with, but it cuts into your profit margin. Sudden repairs will also take time out of your life to handle, cost you money to pay for them, and further affect your profitability. Sure, you could pay 10% of the monthly rent to a property manager so it's less hassle for you, but now you're giving up more of your residuals.

All this being said, I am a big believer in owning real estate as an investment, as I have a nice portion of my investment portfolio in real estate. But this is not how I built my residual fortune. Rather, it's what I invest some of my residuals in so my money can grow while I'm sleeping.

Take a look at all the subscriptions you are paying for every month right now. I bet many of you are probably paying monthly for Sirius Radio, Apple Music or Spotify, cable TV, Netflix, insurance policies of all types, and maybe even a gym membership. These businesses are raking in residual income from you and all of their customers every month. If you can find a way to bring value to consumers by solving a problem in their lives, and do it on a subscription basis, you have hit the jackpot. The subscription model is my absolute favorite. Any time you can get a customer to sign up to buy ANYTHING on a regular ongoing basis, that is the *ultimate* business model.

I made my fortune selling a monthly legal plan. For a tiny monthly fee, people get access to a whole host of legal services paid for via a mobile app. So when they want to call and get help, get their will done for free, handle a speeding ticket, etc., they can easily do so. It's a monthly subscription for only $25. Every month, I earn residual income on every customer, for his or her life on the service! Pretty cool, huh?

I made millions of dollars from my little home office doing this. I started off part-time, started building my customer base, and over time I grew it to where it replaced my real estate income. So I said goodbye to the grind of my real estate selling career and hello to my residual income lifestyle of time freedom.

Just recently, one of my business partners introduced me to a high-powered real estate broker. After I showed him our business model, he said, "I like what I see, I will get on board and see what I can do… but I already make a million dollars a year."

"That's great," I replied, "but I would rather make $500,000 *residually*, than the way you're making a million right now."

Now, I was only making a point, because I already make more residually than he does on the linear basis. I meant this remark in a non-demeaning way. That's amazing that he has scaled his career to a million-dollar income with serious focus and hard work. I am in awe and impressed.

But here's my perspective. He only looked at the top line instead of fully understanding the *full* cost of his income: Long insane hours, constantly being on call, a payday that's only as good as your last sale, the inability to take time off for as long as you need to, and the joy of seeing deposits showing up passively in your bank account every single day of the week, whether you've sold a house or not. He and others talk about how busy they are. A few decades ago, it became a thing of pride to tell people how busy you are. Their inner voice is saying, "I'm so successful because I'm so busy." But the shine of that statement has worn off. Who wants to be busy like that anymore? My prideful claim is now, "I'm happily successful because I'm *not* busy anymore."

I hope you now more fully understand the power of residual income. Most people I meet say they know what residual income is, but when I ask them if they have any, they say they don't. This simply means they never really understood it, because if they did they would go through a brick wall in order to get some.

Maybe you won't be the next Michael Jackson. Maybe you don't want to build an insurance business. But there are some great ideas on the radar screen for developing your residual empire. I will discuss some of these in a coming chapter. I just want you to do your exploration. Find yourself a side business that has all three forms of income — linear, leveraged, and residual income.

Truth be told, this is my little soapbox moment right now. I would not do anything else the rest of my life if it didn't have leveraged and residual income attached. If 100% of your income comes from 100% of what you do, that's just downright scary. What happens if you get sick, can't work, or want to retire? God forbid you lose your job. What would happen? But if you've got leveraged income and residual income, it's not even predicated on you doing any work any more. You can still keep on getting paid.

THOUSANDS MORE REASONS

As if the direct financial benefits weren't enough, there are tax implications that also work in your favor when you start your own business. This equates to more dollars in your pocket and less in Uncle Sam's coffers. As an employee, the government takes a percentage of every dollar you earn. If you make $100,000, they take their cut on that entire amount.

As a business owner, even as a small home-based business owner, if you earn $100,000 you get to write off all of your business expenses *first*, and then pay taxes based on the lowered amount.

Just to give you one example, let's consider a 20-mile errand you run in your vehicle while building your business. Perhaps you need to drive to meet a prospective business partner in a nearby town. If you had driven those miles as a W2 employee, you would have absorbed the full cost of the spent gas and the wear and tear on your vehicle. But the minute you become a business owner, Uncle Sam absorbs that cost for you!

In the U.S., as of this writing, you are allowed a 58-cent allowance per mile for mileage used in the course of conducting your business. So, in the case of our example, driving 20 miles would have allowed you to write off $11.60 from taxes you would have normally owed the government. And that's just one item you're allowed to write off!

Two-thirds of Americans would struggle to scrounge up $1,000 in an emergency.

Source: The Associated Press

You get to write off a whole menu of other expenses, such as:

- Part of your mortgage/rent (home office expense)

- Part of your utilities at your home

- Meals

- Trips

- Supplies

- Phone/internet.

Of course you start your business in pursuit of profits. But in addition to making money, you are also able to save money. A typical home-based business owner can save thousands of in-pocket tax savings each year. Heck, if I didn't already have my own thriving home-based business right now, I would surely start one for this one reason alone!

No time to build a side business?

You can make time if you want to!

Build your empire!

3 PATHS TO BECOMING AN ENTREPRENEUR

L et's talk about the three possible paths you can take to start a business. The first one is you invent something. Are you an inventor? Do you have some great ideas floating around in your head? The challenge with being an inventor is it's high risk and high return. Most inventors lose their money. Most inventors never get their invention off the ground. It takes a ton of capital to fund taking an idea from concept to actually bringing it to market and making money. Most people don't have the ability to give it a go, and a majority of people who do come up with the capital end up losing it all. If it does succeed, it may have a high payoff potential if you have the right profit margins, brand, management, market conditions, etc. An inventor takes big risk.

The second option you have is to buy into a *franchise*. A franchise is a proven business. It's already got a proven model. Other people are already out there doing it and making some money. It's low risk, but it's also a capped limited return. You're going to put up X amount of money and you're going to get a predictable return back. You're probably going to have to invest anywhere from $100,000 to $500,000 of start-up capital to be able to generate maybe $50,000 to $100,000 a year of income off of that one location. A franchisee has much lower risk, but also has a low return potential. Likewise, the sweat equity is predominately yours. You will put in long hours every day to ensure the success of the business.

The third — and what I feel is the absolute best option — is a home-based marketing business, because it's got low to no risk, but super high return potential. There are very successful companies that have products or services they are bringing to the marketplace, and they allow people to become independent small business owners and to build their own businesses marketing these services. These are fully operational companies with products people find valuable, but they just need the marketing/sales end on the ground to generate the sales. Because you have a proven model that's already succeeding in the marketplace, there's not much start-up capital to get it going, and the upside potential is unlimited. Why? Because it's so scalable.

So let's recap: You *invent* something, it's high-risk, high-return — if it works out. A *franchise* incorporates low risk for a limited return, but it's going to take a lot of startup capital to get it going. A *home-based business* in the marketing space affords a low-risk and unlimited income potential.

I chose the third option for myself and it was a massive success. That's why I believe that option is the best chance of success for you as well.

Here are some words to live by that, hopefully, you'll never forget:

Whoever solves the biggest problems for the most people makes the most money.

Your goal right now should be to find a company that's solving a major problem that many people have, and if that company has a proven track record, and if you can believe in the product and its value, then allow yourself to get excited about it. But here's a word of caution: You'll often find that even though *you* got excited about your next endeavor, your friends and family won't always share the same enthusiasm.

When you buy somebody's opinion, you buy their lifestyle. So let me warn you right now: When you make the decision to start your own business, all your W2-employed friends are going to come out of the woodwork and tell you that you're nuts. Unless you want the lifestyle that they've settled for, don't pay attention to their opinions. There's something magical about the feeling of building your own empire. Even if you only have 30 minutes to an hour a day to spend on it, you're going to feel a new exuberance for life because you now know you're building something for you and your family instead of always making someone else rich.

Becoming an entrepreneur gives you the best of all worlds together. You start off part-time, which does not interfere with your job or your busy time schedule. You already have linear income, but now you're adding leveraged income and residual income to your life by going the home business route with little to no risk, and having unlimited upside earning potential.

THE BUSINESS THAT MADE ME TENS OF MILLIONS

You may choose to discredit or ignore this chapter based on your pre-formed or pre-conceived notions. I don't blame you; how do we blame anyone for believing information that's been fed to them by others over a long period of time? I pride myself on being willing to learn new things. A long time ago my own notions challenged what I'm about to share with you. I found that after doing real investigation, my ignorance was based on simply lacking knowledge or being misinformed. I chose to get into the network marketing model for the business education, mentorship, friends, associations, leverage, and passive/residual income. I have seen many business owners whose business owned them. That's not *my* end game!

I have nothing to gain by convincing you to appreciate or agree with my findings here. I'm not trying to recruit you into anything or to sell you anything. If you jump into a negative headspace about an entire industry, you might just miss the life change you're after.

I know what you may be thinking: Network marketing is a "pyramid," isn't it? This is the very belief I had many years ago. When you don't know, you don't know. I was ignorant about this business model when I was first exposed to it. I believed the "pyramid" thing. How did I form this opinion? Simple — I heard someone else say it. Then I repeated it as if it were fact. You know why? Because that's what we do, right? Challenge yourself on this. Have you ever done it? I bet you have. Somewhere along the line before someone told me that network marketing was a "pyramid," they heard it from someone else.

If you could trace it back, someone inevitably has a negative story. Someone got started in a network marketing business and it went south. Maybe the product turned out to be not so good. Maybe the company didn't make it past start-up phase (like many companies don't) and went out of business and left them high and dry. Maybe their sponsor made promises of easy riches that left them with high expectations that were never met. Maybe they recruited a few people who did nothing and thus gave up themselves. In any event, that person has a story of hard feelings towards the experience and they keep perpetually telling the sob story and selling others on why the whole business model is to blame.

What I found as the truth, though, is that there are some amazing network marketing companies out there within which you can become an entrepreneur and start your business and prosper. Maybe you were the one who had a bad experience in such a business before and you've got a bad taste in your own mouth.

Let's look at an analogy of this. Let's say you fall in love and get married. A few years later, you figure out that it isn't working out, for whatever reason. Maybe he/she cheated on you. Your marriage is done. Does that mean the entire institution of marriage is bad? Just because you picked the wrong person to connect with, I hope you wouldn't throw the baby out with the bath water. You had good reason to want to find a partner to be with. Maybe you didn't want to be lonely, or you wanted to share your life with someone who could make you feel complete. We have great reasons for wanting to get married. If it doesn't work out after trying hard to make it work, you can try again. It's common and accepted that you move on and heal, and try again.

So why did you or that person start a network marketing business in the first place? Maybe your job wasn't providing you with the opportunity to get ahead financially. Maybe you had no time freedom due to a hectic work schedule and a rough daily commute. Maybe you were missing your kids growing up because you were always working and you saw people in network marketing businesses working from home making amazing income, while being present with their kids and living a happier life.

We often lose sight of *why* we start something, and when something goes wrong, we just walk away from it and blame an entire business model. Of course, this sounds crazy. Why would anyone think this way?

I don't know, but years ago that was me.

How did my head get turned around to begin appreciating the network marketing business model? Here's my story.

I was programmed my entire life that multilevel marketing, as it's often referred to, was illegal, and people called them "pyramid schemes." So when I was introduced to them over the years, I shut them down and actually lambasted people for bothering me with such nonsense.

I grew up in real estate my entire life. My father built one of the largest real estate brokerage companies on the East Coast in the 1970s, before selling it to Merrill Lynch. When my brother and I graduated from college, we both joined him in building a new real estate company. I went into sales and into opening a few offices, while my older brother went into management of the company.

In sales, I was able to create a six-figure income. I worked 60+ hours a week in such pursuit. My brother worked hard as well, but not in the same fashion. He focused on opening offices and recruiting others as agents to sell houses for him. My brother never listed and sold a single house in his career, yet he eventually out-earned me 10-to-1. He (and my parents) made millions because he earned a cut of every commission from all the houses his 1,000+ agents sold. He worked smarter, while I worked harder. I guess he was at the top of the pyramid.

Is this legal? Should he be allowed to earn more than any of the agents who worked so hard selling homes? I imagine everyone will agree that being a real estate broker is totally legal. Those who are smart, willing to take the financial risk of overhead, and up for the challenge of recruiting good agents are the very ones who get to live a life benefitting from leveraged income.

So how is network marketing any different? I submit to you that I found it to be significantly better.

One day, a friend shared with me how he was earning the same income I was, but that he was doing so from home without the overhead, employees, insurance, stress, or being subject to market conditions. He was doing so in a network marketing business. At first I rebuffed him by telling him that he was in a pyramid scheme. He asked me to explain why. I said that he was earning money off the backs of others he recruited into his downline, not from his own efforts.

"Do you mean like how *your* family earns money off the backs of the real estate agents in your company?" he nonchalantly replied.

I froze, and anyone who knows me knows I am normally quick-witted.

"Who is working smarter, you or your dad and brother?" he asked.

Now I was mad — not at him — but at myself. That was my light bulb moment. I had been closed-minded and it was costing me. This was the birth of my enlightenment, and I began to enter and study the network marketing profession.

My research led me to learn why the business model made so much sense for a company that wanted a cost-effective way to bring a product to market. Instead of spending millions in traditional media ad buys, which has a declining effectiveness, companies were opting to employ the network marketing model. In doing so, the company only incurs marketing cost if and when a sale is made. They get an army of word-of-mouth salespeople using the most effective way of influencing buying decisions, and they only get paid for performance. No salaries, only commissions. But what is also employed is a high sense of motivation, wherein these salespeople can build a business of their own and not just be salespeople.

If they choose to recruit others and teach them how to sell the product or service, then they can earn override income just like the broker in a real estate company does. So now they see life through a different lens, as business owners waking up each day excited about the future they are building for themselves. They are not salespeople, they are business *owners*.

Let's relate this back to my real estate background. Our family built and owned a very large national real estate franchise. They did not work *for* Prudential. On the contrary, they built their own company within the umbrella of that great national, household name and support structure.

In a network marketing business, you are doing the same thing: building your own business within the umbrella of the company you partner with. The marketing team you build is yours. The customer base you build with your team is yours. You have rights to the cash flow generated from your business into perpetuity.

In real estate, the agents will not likely be able to out-earn the big broker they work for. Their income is limited to only what they can personally generate. The broker is able, through massive leverage in hiring many agents, to earn substantial override commissions. How could one agent compete with that? But nowadays, many real estate companies have caught onto the merits of multilevel marketing.

Instead of only one top broker earning commissions off all the homes being sold by the agents they recruited, some brokers have now elicited the help of their agents to re-cruit more agents to grow their company. Agents can re-cruit other agents and get overrides on their sales, with-out being the broker at the top and without footing the massive overhead bill.

In essence, they can create their own "downline" network of agents within the existing structure. Some of the fastest growing brokerages have employed this model and it is the reason for their significant growth. Why? The agents would rather not just earn from only their own sales. They want *leveraged income.*

Circling back to my story, I decided to start a network mar-keting business on the side of my 60-hour-a-week real es-tate career. I only had a few hours a week I could devote, but I did just that. At first, I didn't earn great sums of money, but I did learn a great deal. The entrepreneurial education I gained from the experience was far bigger than the initial earnings I generated.

But in time, my earnings grew as I grew within the profes-sion. Presently, my monthly income from network market-ing is more than I used to make *annually* in real estate.

Top that off with the fact that my income is now 97% passive overrides and residual income from the customer base that has been built! Passive, residual income grants me the freedom to be a stay-at-home dad, to travel, and to feel in control. Now that I have lived in both worlds — traditional business and network marketing — I will *never* go back. Network marketing is the only way I can see for average people like me to get ahead and get control of our lives.

A LESSON FROM THE REAL ESTATE INDUSTRY

So let me give you an example of the power of using the network marketing business model in a traditional business you're likely familiar with. You know that a real estate agent gets paid a commission for selling your house. The more houses they sell, the more money they make. Straightforward and simple.

Now some agents decide they want to become brokers and hire other agents to go sell houses for them. Every time an agent sells a house, the agent gets paid a percentage of the commission and the broker gets paid a percentage. Why should the broker get a percentage? It's because the broker is bringing value to the agents working under him. The broker provides training, support, brand equity and name recognition, guidance in closing deals, leverage with economies of scale in buying supplies and tools, technology platforms, and more. The agent on his or her own would not be able to afford all of this, and certainly in the beginning would be lost without the advice, guidance, and support.

Keller Williams became one of the fastest growing real estate brokerages in the world in recent years. How did they do it? They looked at the traditional way a real estate brokerage was built. Someone decided to become a broker, then that person started hiring agents into the first office. Once the office was humming along, the broker would open another office, hire an office manager, and that manager would be tasked with filling the office with agents. The manager would be the only recruiter, and the incentive would be in earning a percentage off every deal done by agents in that office. So the manager would usually sit in his office making calls trying to convince agents that this was a better office to work out of and explain some of the advantages in the attempt to recruit them.

Here's the challenge. The manager is not out there in the market doing deals with the other agents. It's the agents who are negotiating with the other agents, and forming relationships. When a broker or manager calls an agent to try to recruit them, the agents typically would blow them off. There was no preexisting relationship basis first.

Keller Williams solved the riddle. They decided to leverage the relationships all of their agents had with fellow agents in the marketplace. They implemented a network marketing model, which is relationship marketing. If an agent called up a colleague and convinced them, based on their own great experience at Keller Williams, to move their license over to work at KW, every time the recruited agent sells a house the recruiter got paid an override (just like the broker at the top does).

Can you imagine how well this worked? If you were an agent working in KW, why would you want to recruit others to come there too and become competition for you? Here's why: *You get paid every time they sell a house!* So you would want to recruit as many agents as you could for the firm, right? Of course you would! And you'd want those agents to be super successful, right? Of course you would, because you got paid when they succeeded!

So, in effect, the company grew because the agents grew it for them. And the agents love it because they could have the benefits of getting paid passive override income without the expense and risk of founding their own brokerage. They get to leverage a strong brand name, create a brokerage within a brokerage if you will, and enjoy the spoils.

And wouldn't you know it, the environment inside KW became one of the most fun, uplifting places to work one's real estate career. This is because everyone wanted everyone to succeed. They stopped looking at each other as competition and instead spent their energy supporting each other. Keller Williams grew by thousands and thousands of new agents joining the company each year. This is not just a great real estate success story, it's a testament to the power and effectiveness of the network marketing business model. And currently *eXp Realty* has used a next generation model of this and has grown to more than 18,000 agents in just a few short years.

The owners figured out that it's the agents who know the other agents out there. So they incentivize them to help recruit those agents. They get paid to sell houses, and also as recruiters to help grow the company. So is real estate brokerage a pyramid? Of course not! You can employ this same model to sell virtually anything — nutritional supplements, services, educational products, or anything else.

Now you might still disagree with me and hold tight to your belief that network marketing is somehow bad. It's just a difference in philosophy or value system. You may only value working for linear income, getting paid on only what you do. Maybe to you, working hard every day indefinitely is a virtue. You may think you're right, and to you and your value system, you *are* right. But you can be "broke right."

Did you ever hear of being "dead right" crossing at a crosswalk? This is what my mom always used to warn me of as a young boy. She said to always cross at a crosswalk, because by law cars must give a pedestrian the right of way. But she said to never trust that a car is going to see you and stop as you cross. If you feel like it's your legal right to cross the street and if car hits you it's their fault, you'd be right. But you'd be dead, too. Hence, you'd be "dead right," and that's hardly the outcome you would want.

So maybe your value system places much value on working for a paycheck. Maybe you want to hold onto that story someone put in your head that network marketing and leveraged income is no good.

Let's just say you're convinced that your line of thinking is absolutely right. I ask you in all humility: how's that thinking working out for you? If it was working, you'd have complete and utter time freedom, you'd be debt free with plenty of money to fund your dream lifestyle, and you'd be genuinely happy spending all the time you want with your spouse, kids, and friends. But I know for a fact — not only statistically speaking, but through experience from coaching thousands of people into becoming successful entrepreneurs — that most people trading their time for a paycheck at a job are not living that way.

The good news is that such a scenario is only one mental shift away for you. Once you open your mind to learning the benefits of a better business model, then and only then, do you have a chance to make the shift and gain your freedom.

INCOME DISCLOSURE

You may be thinking, "But hardly anybody makes money in those home based businesses." Well, you might think that because you don't have any immediate friends who have made a fortune in this business model. But that doesn't mean thousands of people aren't enjoying incredible success. I know this as fact because I have met and have taught tons of such success stories.

But let's pause on this for a minute. If you believe that hardly anyone hits it big in a network marketing business, I assure you that such is the case in *every* industry out there. Did you know that more than 80% of people who get a real estate license never sell one house? They spent the money and time to get licensed, had visions of success, but then, nothing. Does that mean you cannot make money selling houses? Of course not. Some people do incredibly well.

Just remember that there is an 80/20 rule in every industry (and in every endeavor on earth!), and human nature will never change. Eighty percent of people who start down *any* path do very little, while 20% go do the work and make 80% of the money. Of the 20%, there will always be the outliers

— the achievers who are the most ambitious and are recognized as the top earners in that space. What separates the top achievers from the rest? They are just more determined and focused, and more consistent and urgent in their efforts than everybody else.

So here is my income disclosure: Great success story results are not typical, and that is simply because people who start businesses and actually stick with them to the point of success are not typical. Most people do little, or quit, which is why people think you cannot make money in a home-based business.

Here's the fix for that: *Choose not to be "most people!"*

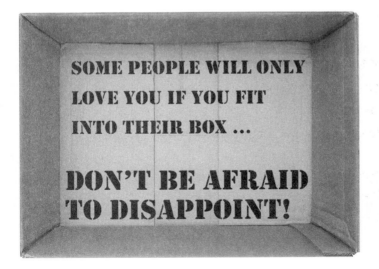

SOME PEOPLE WILL ONLY
LOVE YOU IF YOU FIT
INTO THEIR BOX ...

DON'T BE AFRAID
TO DISAPPOINT!

LIVE OUTSIDE OF "THE BOX"

Figuratively (someone else's design for you) *and* ... *Literally* (an office or cubicle).

You may have spent much of your life living by other people's rules. We all sure did in school. And in the workplace, we are told when to be at work, when we can leave, how many days we are allowed to be sick, and when we can take a vacation. As employees, we have to adapt and adopt the culture of the company. We are not in control. We don't call the shots. We have to check our creative ideas at the doors. After all, it's not our company.

Control, flexibility and creativity are three of the great attributes you'll find when building your own business. *You* get to control how fast or slow you build. *You* decide the pace you want to grow it, and how much effort to devote to it. *You* get to have complete flexibility in scheduling your business around your life, whereas you might be used to having to schedule you life around your work.

Because it is *your* business, *you* call the shots. *You* can bring your creative flair to everything you do. You no longer have to conform to whatever company culture you've ever been a part of.

YOU CANNOT QUIT ON YOURSELF

One of the hardest things about making the shift to becoming an entrepreneur is that nobody can make you stay with it and see your business through to success. You alone control your own destiny. And that is a hard thing! Especially when most of the people in your life are trying to keep you in the same box they are in. It's like crabs in a bushel basket. You take the lid off, and the crabs on top try to climb out to freedom, but the ones underneath grab them with their claws to hold them down. That is exactly what your friends and family will often do when you decide to go down this path. And due to this peer pressure you will be very tempted to quit and go back to the life you are used to.

Remember, nothing worthwhile is ever easy. And if becoming a super successful entrepreneur was easy, everyone would do it. Everyone would be wealthy. If everyone had a million dollars, than a million wouldn't have much value. So don't want what you don't want. Embrace the process and appreciate that it's going to be hard at times, but always remember the juice will be worth the squeeze.

This quote from the legendary business mogul, coach, and author Grant Cardone makes an important point:

Rest assured, you're not a bad person. You aren't even a hater ...
you're a quitter.

You watch the lifestyle I've created, the work ethic, the family life, the endless production of new content, the willingness to take new risks and the insatiable appetite to create success at new levels.

You criticize and find fault with what I'm doing. But you don't hate me and you're not envious of me. The reality is you quit doing what you see me doing and it kills you.

And the crazy thing is you could have probably done it better, and said it more professionally, and written it more poetically. But you didn't — instead, you QUIT. So the next time you want to criticize me or have some critical thought of me, remember, it's not because you're a hater,
it's because you are a QUITTER.

Haters – by Grant Cardone

This is deep. It is the truth.

In my business, anyone could've done what I did (and still can) and likely better than me. But most quit when it got tough. Most quit because it was hard. Most didn't focus and put in the work because they were seeking the myth called "balance." Who determines what balance is? Balance is a farce.

You do what you want to do and what makes you happy. If being an entrepreneur and creating massive success makes you happy, and allows you to live the life of your dreams because of it, then that's your *balance*. If happiness is spending equal amounts of time in each area of your life, and that is balance to you, you can work hard to achieve that.

I have watched countless people quit. They justify that because they are "so busy." Busy doing *what*? Certainly not busy doing what makes them happy. Certainly not building towards an end game of utter freedom. They are busy scurrying around living a life designed for them by some matrix that all these other mindless people are following. "I'm just playing the hand I've been dealt," they say. That's sad. Don't they know they can discard and get new cards?

The fact that network marketing allows any person the flexibility to get started and grow their business while still working a job or traditional business (that often owns them) is a gift from above. Embrace it. There is no excuse now.

Start by admitting that you bought other people's opinions, and, hence, bought their lifestyles. If they don't live the life you want, why care what they think? If they aren't willing to focus on building a bright future and would rather focus their energies on working hard for someone else and to convince themselves they are happy, it's a shame you'd choose to follow suit.

Success is a choice, a decision. I hope today you'll decide you're going to create a business plan, and stick with that plan with more focus and burning desire than ever in your life — because your quality of life depends on it.

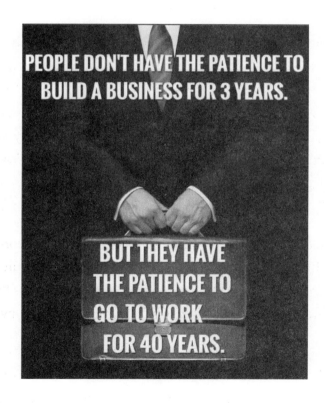

REASONS PEOPLE DON'T SUCCEED

Black Bart was a professional thief who terrorized the Wells Fargo stage line between 1875 and 1883. The very utterance of his name struck fear in people's hearts. During that eight-year period, Bart robbed 29 different stagecoach crews. From San Francisco to New York, his very presence symbolized the danger of the frontier. Incredibly he did all of this without firing a single shot. He also never took a single hostage or actually caused harm to anyone. How?

Because Bart used a hood to hide his face, no victim ever saw his face. Instead, Black Bart used *fear* to paralyze his victims. His sinister presence was enough to overwhelm the toughest stagecoach guard.

If you think the fear factor was relegated to the Wild Frontier, you'd be grossly mistaken. The truth of the matter is that *fear* always has — and always will — dictate people's decisions, regardless of how rational or irrational that fear may be. Stock markets rise and fall based on fear. Nations attack other nations based on fear. Overprotective parents extinguish their kids' creative sparks based on fear. It goes on and on.

The thought of starting a business can be daunting at first. There are so many uncertainties and so many logistics to think through. And if you're predisposed to fear to begin with, it can start you down a spiral of fear that will torpedo your business before it ever leaves the ground.

In fact, fear is the number one reason that people don't succeed in life. Unfortunately, fear has many facets. In business, giving into any *one* of them can put you into the liability column very quickly. Part of starting your own business is to know in advance the fears that are likely to rear their ugly heads — and to defeat them before they settle in.

Here are the top reasons I've seen people fail in business — and in life.

FEAR OF FAILURE

Who likes to fail? Nobody. Everyone fears failure. We don't want to experience failure, because we sometimes define ourselves by it. We feel that other people will look at us as a failure. For self-preservation purposes, many people decide not to even start a business because they don't want to look bad in the eyes of the world, or even in the mirror. It's so much easier to stay down on the ground with the rest of your friends where everyone is used to you being, rather than to try flying high and have everyone betting on when you'll come crashing back into the crowd below.

FEAR OF SUCCESS

Who wants to succeed? Everyone! Who wants *you* to succeed? Not the people you would think, sadly. Right now, the people you hang around are mostly all in the same boat. Everyone in your circle likely works long hours, makes the same kind of money, and has the same struggles. Basically they are all in the same trapped scenario in one form or another. But *what if* you decide to start a business and you hit your homerun?

You are now quitting your job, spending time with your family, traveling, moving into a new home, and upgrading your life. You are subconsciously worried about how those friends will now perceive you.

"Look at her, she thinks she's hot stuff now. She doesn't have time for us anymore, always going on vacations, driving that new Mercedes, hanging out with her new rich friends. She thinks she's better than us now."

They are naturally going to be jealous.

They could do what you did, but they choose to stay exactly where they are, and how dare you go out there and succeed and make them look bad? They may or may not say it, but subconsciously some will think it. But you cannot choose to hold your life down because you're afraid that your success will make others feel like failures. This fear of success is real for many people and they don't even realize it. They will often sabotage their own success so that they can keep themselves down with the flock of chickens pecking around on the ground rather than soaring with the eagles. Don't do this to yourself.

FEAR OF BEING TOO BUSY

Being too busy causes some people to not start a side business. And very often, those who do start a business will end up letting the business sit idle and vanish because they feel their life is too busy to build it. Therefore they seal their fate to keep them stuck right where they are. If you ever want to get "unbusy," you have to make the time for your business to succeed. Here's truth: Everyone is busy. Everyone. You'll rarely, if ever, meet someone who says, "Gee, I have so much time on my hands. Now would be the *best* time for me to start a business!" Everyone is busy, but true success depends on how you mitigate that busy-ness and parlay it into a victory for you and your family.

FEAR OF REJECTION

In any business, you have to go out and build it. You have to sell something in the marketplace, whether it's a product or a service. Rest assured, not everyone will say "Yes" and become a customer. Not everyone you want to hire to come work for you or recruit into the business will see your vision. Go into it knowing this, or else the first five no's might knock you right off your horse. When you take a peek behind the curtain of every successful person, you will *always* find examples of rejection. Steve Jobs, Elvis Presley, J.K. Rowling, Steven King, Abraham Lincoln, The Beatles, Marilyn Monroe, Steven Spielberg, Walt Disney, Oprah Winfrey, and even Jesus Christ, were rejected during the process of trying to make their mark. I don't think I need to remind anyone that every one of them ended up changing the world. The fear of rejection is only as powerful your willingness to embrace it.

FEAR THAT IT WON'T GO AS PLANNED

Every start-up entrepreneur has a vision for the business they are about to build. They spent time planning it all out, and have big expectations. But this is not a scratch-off lottery ticket. The first few action steps you take most likely will not yield the results you are expecting. Some people may quit on you. The market may change and you may need to pivot. In fact, the only certainly in this world is uncertainty! The truth is, your endeavor probably *won't* go exactly the way you envisioned it. There are too many moving parts, too many personalities, too many external factors that are likely to throw you a curveball. But if you keep your heading to true north and not allow yourself to be stripped of your dream, you *will* be successful!

FEAR OF LEAVING THE PACK AND GOING IT ALONE

Are you afraid of feeling lonely? It is common for entrepreneurs to feel isolated, because you're no longer a part of a pack of employees. Misery loves company, and sometimes you may be tempted to stay in the misery because that's where all your friends are. Also the entrepreneur has to do many things alone: from decision-making, to handling problems, reinventing the product, creating the vision for the company, and driving the business — all of this is now your responsibility. To some people, the fear of added responsibility never allows them to leave the launching pad.

FEAR OF LETTING GO OF THE STEADY PAYCHECK

Job security and predictable income is an addiction. I love what *Rich Dad, Poor Dad* author Robert Kiyosaki says: "If you still believe in job security, you probably still believe in the Easter Bunny!" There really is no more job security. Even the U.S. government just recently furloughed 800,000 workers with no pay for weeks. Do you think your company won't replace you with someone younger, faster, and cheaper sometime soon? That "steady" paycheck is only going to get you by, pay your bills, and keep you living check to check. That's the very essence of this book — to help you come to grips with saying goodbye to that dependency existence.

FEAR THAT YOU WON'T BE GOOD AT IT

Becoming a success in anything takes time. You have to be willing to be bad before you're good at anything. This is true in sports, in music, in games, and in business. If you give up too soon, how will you ever get good and win? In fact, give yourself permission from the onset that you probably *won't* be very good at your endeavor in the beginning. Take the pressure off and set the proper expectation. But remember that the road to mastery of *anything* is paved with inexperience, mistakes, and a steep learning curve in the beginning. Keep doing it. You *will* get better.

FEAR OF LEARNING SOMETHING NEW

If you don't learn something new, then you'll never get new results and create a new lifestyle. You have to be willing to be coachable, have a burning desire, and be willing to work. Most people want to be done with that after their last day of school. Few people ever read a book when it is not required of them. The fact that you are reading this book already separates you from the crowd. Embrace the new lingo, the new connections, the new culture you'll be exposed to, and the new adventure that lies ahead of you. Absorb all you can to give yourself an inextinguishable edge.

FEAR OF CONFLICTS WITH OTHERS IN THE BUSINESS

Can you imagine making a decision to start a business to change your entire life and then you decide to walk away from it just because you get into an argument with someone in your business? Well, you might not be able to fathom this, but I see it happen all the time. Your business success has to be so large and important to you that nothing will derail your mission. Don't convince yourself in advance that something may or may not happen in the future. By doing so, you're giving yourself an out before you ever really got in.

FEAR OF COMPETITION

Competition is a good thing. It makes you always strive to get better and stay out in front. David took down Goliath. There are countless stories of the little company coming along and dethroning the king of that market. Look how a guy like Jeff Bezos decided to take on the huge book stores and sell books online via his little startup, Amazon. The competition tried to knock him out, but he persisted. As of this writing, he is the wealthiest man in the world, with a net worth of $155 billion. Bezos had a vision, and his vision continued to evolve and grow. It's his being sold on his own vision that kept him going, eventually getting millions of customers sold on his company.

There are surely many other reasons I am not describing that cause people to not start a business of their own, or to quit the ones they started. You just have to be bigger than them all. Your vision must be self-inspiring, and your determination iron-clad.

At a job you can complain about a boss' decision. When it's your business, you have to take the blame yourself, and that's not easy. People are used to seeking easy and to doing as little as they can to get paid as much as the company will pay. As an entrepreneur, you have to do way more work, often not getting paid for it in the beginning so that later you'll get paid without having to work for it. But most people don't get this.

49% of Americans are "concerned, anxious or fearful about their current financial well-being."

Source: MarketWatch

Take a look at the chart on the next page. You will do a ton of work in the beginning and you will get paid less than you wish in those beginning months or years, so that later on you will be getting paid a ton of money for time you no longer have to spend. This chart is *the reason* that I was willing to stick with my decision in the early days of my business when the income wasn't where I wanted it to be. Because I didn't quit, and because I just kept planting the seeds and cultivating over and over, the harvest of the millions of dollars did come to fruition.

INVEST TIME TO GET A BIG RETURN

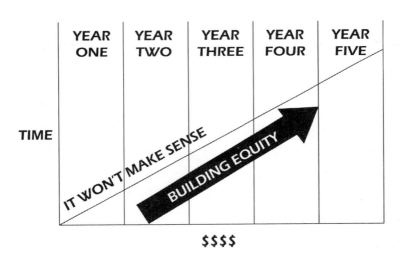

They only way to fail is to quit.
If you don't quit, you can never fail.

KEY TO SUCCESS – FINDING GOOD MENTORS

Come up with who your dream mentor would be, and find a way to get around him/her and learn.

This is the hack for success as an entrepreneur. Instead of spending 20 years going through all the tribulations learning all of the hard knock lessons yourself, just go learn from people who have already been through it all. They will show you the pitfalls and how to avoid them based on real-life solutions and strategies they discovered. They will share with you their best practices that will help you be more efficient and effective, and will accelerate your results. Having a great mentor can help you get to the top of your business game in a third of the time it might have taken you on your own. And frankly, I'd even say that *without a mentor it's highly probable you may never even get to the top.*

Another benefit of having great mentors is the confidence it gives you. You go forward on your journey knowing you have experts who are guiding your steps. Should you find yourself in a deep rut, or encounter a pitfall or obstacle, you know that a mentor is a phone call away to help you navigate it.

How do you find a mentor like this? *This is the million-dollar question.* There are some tremendously knowledgeable and successful people out there in your field, but most of them are out of your league. They are super busy, super successful, and super hard to connect with, much less to get them to notice you and take you under their wing. Even if you offered to pay them for their time for mentorship, you couldn't afford the great ones.

Imagine how much it would cost to have John Legend as your singing coach for voice lessons. Maybe $100,000 per hour? Imagine Richard Branson on starting or running a business? Maybe $200,000 an hour? Maybe Grant Cardone on building a productive sales team? Or the #1 real estate agent for raising your real estate game? Or Warren Buffett on investing? Or Michael Jordan on basketball? Or Tiger Woods on golf? Or Elon Musk on technology? First, good luck getting past the gatekeepers to reach any of these people. Even if you did, when you propose that you'd like to hire them as your personal mentor, even with the .0001% chance they would say yes, you would have to borrow money from the Federal Reserve to pay for that!

Of all the examples above, probably the most inexpensive person to find and hire might be the top real estate agent in the country. But let's think this through.

Let's say his name is Jeff Homes. Why would Jeff want to spend his extremely valuable time helping teach you? Because he's a really nice guy? Come on, if you aren't his niece or nephew, there isn't a chance that he's nice enought to give away his most precious commodity. Maybe you're willing to pay him a generous sum, say $100,000? You might have Jeff's attention with that. He may calculate that he will allow you several hours to let you pick his brain and gain some insights for that. But think deeper. Will Jeff give you all of his secrets to success? If he does, and you are a competitor in the marketplace, he just gave away his secret sauce so that you can now cannibalize his customers and take his market share. Will he really be willing to do that for a tiny morsel of a payment you offer for it? I highly doubt it.

You see, in many industries, the best got there first because they figured out a secret sauce that they don't want their competitors to learn. And they just outworked, sacrificed, and focused more consistently than anyone else.

Is this real talk getting you down about finding a mentor to help you get to the top of the mountain of success? You're probably thinking, "Gee, I thought this book was going to inspire me! You're telling me how important it is to find a mentor, yet it sounds impossible to find one. What gives?"

I'm simply sharing with you that learning from others is crucial. Of course it's very unlikely you'll get to have the number one person in any field become your personal coach and friend. But you can always seek out the highest level person you can find in that space who *is* available to someone like you, at a more manageable price. Just be aware of the give-and-take. If they were *really* great at that endeavor, they likely would not spend their time coaching others — they'd rather still be doing it themselves. As they say, "Those who can't ... teach."

But I have discovered the one place where you can find a mentor who wants to help you, where someone else pays them to help you, and they would actually love to see you take every drop of knowledge they have in them and go tear up the world! *How is this possible?* you may ask. Doesn't this go against everything I just said in the preceding paragraphs? The reason I can confidently state this as a fact is because I lived it!

I was introduced to a business model where there is a true alignment of interests. The people who are already super successful are willing to take you under their wing as a part of their team, develop you into a successful business owner and leader, and take you from caterpillar to majestic butterfly. When you are out in the marketplace acquiring customers and enlarging your footprint, these mentors are happy for you and for themselves, because your success is *their* success. This is because this business model compensates them from your success that they helped you achieve.

This money to compensate them does not even come out of

your earnings, but rather it is above-the-line money paid to them by company profits. So you get the best scenario you can ever dream up! You find the Michael Jordan or the Warren Buffett in that space/business, you work to build your own business under their umbrella of tutelage, and when you win, they win. The more you earn, the more they earn. If they hold back their secret sauce it costs them big.

I had to grapple with this for a bit because it seemed too good to be true. But the more I evaluated how brilliantly this business model was set up, the more genius it proved to be. I shared my enthusiasm with a friend of mine about how I had discovered this path to mega-success and that I have these highly successful mentors who were guiding my steps. You know what he said?

"Ha ha! You've gotten into one of those pyramid things!" I asked him what he meant by that. He explained, "Those people above you just recruit you in, take your money, and they make all their money off the little people like you."

Now I couldn't judge him for saying this, because in all honesty, I thought very much along these lines, as you might recall from my previous story of the guy who handed me my lunch when I tried using the same argument with him.

So I asked, "Do you mean that it's not fair that the top people in the company are making more income than I am?"

"Not necessarily," he answered. "The people above me in my company make more than me."

"So that's fair, right?" I replied. "They have paid their dues, they've worked their way up, and they command a bigger income. You have every opportunity to do the same. You can climb your way to the top of your company too, right?"

"Well, yes and no," he said awkwardly. "I can get promoted and earn more, to a degree. I don't see myself ever becoming the president of the company, obviously. It's not my company and I'm not a part of the owner's family."

"That's true," I agreed. "In the corporate world, you get paid more the more value you bring to the company, but there are most always glass ceilings you bump up against and that's as far as you go. So what's the real rub about my mentor I am working under getting paid by the company for helping me build my business?"

"Those businesses only make money by getting people like you to buy in and pay a fee to start up," he quickly stated. "And they convince you to buy their products. That's how they make money off you."

A big smile came across my face. He noticed it right away.

"I totally hear what you're saying. That's what I was thinking, too! Makes sense when looking at it that way. Let me give you some perspective."

I had another friend give a business like this a go and quit soon after. Because I never saw him as a quitter, I just figured the business had to be the problem. That's why when I was introduced to an extremely intelligent and successful entrepreneur who explained this model to me and I got a completely different perspective on it.

"Here is the way the structure is set up," he explained. "The company has a product it wants to acquire customers for. Instead of hiring and paying salespeople, they instead kind of franchise it out. They let people start their own business for themselves within the company umbrella, thus leveraging all the company brand, assets, products, marketing, training and fulfillment. That new business owner can go sell the product and earn commissions. The company only pays when value is brought, meaning when customers are acquired. No customer, no cost. It's the perfect model for the company. And the small business owner has the right to sell as much or as little as they want. It's their business.

"But here's the brilliant next part. The company wants more salespeople, meaning more business owners. But they aren't spending great sums of money advertising and paying headhunters to go find them. They let the happy existing independent business owners they already have go share the news about that same opportunity with others. If they help recruit someone into the company, the company gained another salesperson with no upfront acquisition cost. Brilliant! The company can keep growing because its happy independent 'brokerage' owners are spreading the word and doing the recruiting for them. Word of mouth allows the company to scale and grow so effectively.

"Here's how it's even better. The independent business owner who recruited this new owner into the company now has them as a part of their business team structure, which is the important part. The company has money in the budget to pay the business owner (mentor) who recruited the new person and helped onboard and train them so that they become successful and sell more product/services. When that new person gets paid for acquiring customers, the 'upline' owner/mentor who brought them into the company and helped them learn the ropes also gets paid an override commission on those sales.

"This is brilliant because the company has the most effective selling owners in the field onboarding and mentoring all of the new hires for them! So the people who know how to do it are teaching others to do it. And they aren't worried about those new owners taking away their market share because they will get compensated by the company for it anyway.

"Do you see why this model is so brilliant and way better than the franchise model? The hiring, training, supporting, and selling is done by the people for the people. All the company has to do is create a compensation model where they budget how much they can pay the seller, the seller's upline support people, and still keep a solid profit margin for the company to thrive, to fulfill all the product orders, and innovate new future products. Brilliant!"

Hearing this explanation from a mega-millionaire business tycoon who owned over a dozen companies, employed thousands of people, and owned more real estate than anyone I've ever met, helped me to comprehend how the model is as perfect as you can get.

After this long dissertation I shared with my friend, he said, "That all makes sense. I never thought of it like that. I just thought those companies try to make their money by signing up distributors. I didn't get how the model actually works. So tell me, this mega-millionaire you're learning all this from, how did you find him?"

Ha! You see, this is what I'm saying. I would never have found such mentors in any traditional business model. He would have never had the reason to spend even a minute with me. But because he had started a business within a company using this model, this aligned his interest with helping me learn and succeed in *my* business. This is how I got to be personally and directly mentored by millionaires and even a billionaire. And I didn't have to pay them, thanks to the network marketing model!

I am so glad I got past my preconceived notion that the model is stupid. And now after earning $20+ million in such a business, you're sitting here reading my fourth book! Always remember, your mind is like a parachute — it only works when it's open.

LIVING FOR THE WEEKEND

Are you guilty of this? Just admit it, it's Monday morning and you're thinking you just want to "get through" these next five days and get to Friday afternoon so you can have some fun. I know you've thought like this, because I used to think that way too. There are even song lyrics "Everybody's working for the weekend … " It's the Matrix the masses live in. Wake up, go to work, come home, feed the kids, go to bed to rest so you can wake up, go to work, come home, feed the kids, go to bed to rest so you can wake up, go to work, come home, feed the kids, go to bed to rest so you can …

I get the feeling! That's a heck of a mundane rhythm of life that you *need* the weekends to have something to look forward to.

But, wow, that's five days out of seven you *don't* look forward to? Is what you do for a living so unexciting that you just want to get through it — get past "Hump Day" Wednesday so you can get to Friday and have "Happy Hour?"

Happy hour is designed for those who aren't happy at their jobs to go have some drinks to "take the edge off" and dull the pain of their week. That is a downright shame to spend roughly 70% of your life just working towards getting to the 30%. And what's worse, it's not just for a temporary season of your life.

People are working and living like this for 40 years or longer. Is that what you looked forward to as a young kid who dreamed about doing amazing things with your life? Get a job at a company where you trade away 8-10 hours a day (plus commute) for a paycheck that only comes as long as you keep trading? Only getting to have fun on weekends and maybe a couple of vacations a year? You're OK with this?

You've probably heard people say, "If you follow your passion and do what you love, you will never feel like you're working." Sure, but 90% of people who try to live this axiom end up broke. You know, the "starving artists." Just because you are passionate about something, it doesn't mean it will fulfill your purpose. You might be passionate about playing music, but your *purpose* may be to earn money and provide for your family. I have seen marriages break up because one partner insisted they wanted to "follow their passion" but couldn't make any money at it. And because they weren't carrying their weight financially, their lives caved in.

Most people need to keep their passions as hobbies and find something they can do that will responsibly bring home the bacon and pay for their lifestyle. Is it possible to find something you are totally passionate about that you can also monetize and make a fortune doing? Yes, but these are exceptions, and not at all common. So I absolutely recommend starting there first. Write down the things you truly love to do. Then honestly explore those options to see which, if any, is a viable way for you to succeed financially.

Again, I am assuming that financial success ranks as an important priority in your life. If you think you can succeed at it, I don't recommend burning your ships and just going all in right from here. If you have something you feel you'd love to do and there is money in it, take that path off your hobby list and pursue it as a part-time career with the hope of proving it out as something you can make your full-time calling. In this way, you are not risking financial suicide by quitting your job only to learn this new path of passion is not going to be financially fruitful.

Some of the things I truly love to do are golfing, fishing, surfing, and traveling. Those are things I consider hobbies. I do them as often as I wish, but those are not things I can claim as how I make my bread and butter. My full-time career was as a real estate agent. But I am quite lucky to have found something I am also passionate about that pays *big money.* I love entrepreneurship. I love to build businesses and make money. I love to teach others how to do the same — like writing this book for example. I absolutely *love* what I do. And, man, does it pay well!

The more deeply I fell in love with being an entrepreneur, the more my income climbed. I feel congruent because my goals and purpose in life are in alignment with what I do with my time every day. I wake up every morning – yes, even Monday, Tuesday, Wednesday and Thursday, too — excited about building the empire.

You see, I took Jim Rohn's advice. I kept working in real estate while I was doing my entrepreneurial ventures on the side. Once I found the one that was generating significant income, and as I felt it was something I could truly fall in love with, I pursued it with vigor. I replaced my real estate income, walked away and have never looked back. I now make more in a month than I made in my biggest year in real estate. And I make that passively now. I have real time freedom, meaning I wake up when I want and work when I want. The truth is, I love what I do so much that I look forward to waking up to attack it each day!

I have not worked because I *needed* money for over 15 years. I work because I love what I do, and because I know I can accomplish more amazing goals. I love chasing goals, don't you? It makes me feel alive and excited about life.

BURN YOUR EXCUSES

I've got to say that one of the most fulfilling things in my life was actually not my decision to start a part-time business and develop it into a multi-million dollar empire. It's the chance that I've had to work with countless other people who needed a way to change their lives. They saw an opportunity to start their own part-time business, and to watch them flourish and become successful and see their lives change has meant everything to me.

Never let your reasons to start a part-time business for yourself ever become your excuse not to, because you might be thinking, "You know what? I've been thinking throughout the years about starting a business, but I just don't have time to add something else into my life."

That was my story. *I almost completely missed it. My life almost didn't change.* I was working in my real estate career 50 to 60 hours a week. I had no time for family, and no time for friends. I was always grinding and working, and when I was introduced to a business project that was incredible, I said, "I don't have time for it." Thankfully, the gentleman who introduced it to me did not just say, "OK," and move on. He said, "Brian you seem like you're incredibly busy. Do you like living like that?"

"Well, not really," I replied.

"What makes you think if you keep on doing what you're doing, that five years from now you'll be any less busy than you are today?"

"Well, I don't know. I never thought about it."

"You are so crazy busy. Don't let your reason to start a business that can change all of that be your excuse why you *can't*. If you want time freedom in your life, you've got to find a way to get a passive residual cash flow coming in from a side business so that you can cut back on your real estate hours and start enjoying your life."

"But here's the dilemma ... even if I would love to do that, I don't have time to add a side business into my agenda."

"Brian, just use 'split second marketing.' You can find little slivers of time, and then compound it over the next couple years, and build yourself a great passive income that can set you free."

And that's exactly what happened for me. I've been a stay-at-home dad for my kids' entire lives. I've traveled to 19 different countries. I work from home. Now I've got the best lifestyle I've ever dreamed of. But that almost didn't happen because I almost let my reason to start a part-time business be my excuse *not* to. So that "no time" thing — don't let that be yours!

You might say, "Well, I've got plenty of time, I just don't have the money." That's probably not a good feeling, right? How many years have you been working at your job or jobs? Several years? And you have not saved up a lot of money yet? Of course that's not a good feeling! But if you keep on working several *more* years, is that going to be any different? What I would submit to you is if money is an issue, don't let that be your *excuse* not to start a business. That's got to be a *reason why you've got to* start a business. I know of great businesses you can start on a shoe-string budget of a few hundred dollars. If you don't have that, I bet you could scrape it together if you wanted it bad enough.

You might even be in the camp that says, "Hey look, you know, I personally just don't think I would be cut out for a business. I've never been an entrepreneur. I've always had a job. I've always had a boss telling me what to do, what not to do, and so forth. I'm not sure if I would be good at it."

I have heard that from countless people who had never been entrepreneurs. They've always been W-2 employees. But when we show them word-for-word, step-by-step, how to start a part-time business with little slivers of time a few hours a week, and that they can plug into a proven system and just follow the playbook, I've seen countless people find success. I've watched them blossom and develop into incredible part-time business owners where their incomes were taking off, and gaining time freedom with their families. That would never have happened if they had said, "You know, I just want to play it safe. I want to stick to my job," and never even try to put themselves on a better path.

MONEY IS LIKE WATER

Money, like water, seeks its own level. Water will always keep flowing down as low as it can go. It will seep down in between anything you pour it over. It just wants to go down. That's how money is too. *You will earn who you are.* If you are used to making $60,000 a year at your job, how do you plan to make $200,000? It won't happen just because you want it harder or pray harder for it. You get paid in direct proportion to the value that you bring to the marketplace — the place where the money is. If you want more money, you must bring more value. How do you elevate your value? You become more valuable. You grow yourself; you develop yourself. There are no shortcuts other than learning from mentors who have already done it.

Do you ever notice how so many people who win the lottery are broke 5-10 years later? Just because they got a million dollars doesn't mean they became a millionaire (in their mindset and knowledge). They simply got temporary custody of a million dollars. Soon enough, the money left them because they didn't grow up fast enough to learn how to keep it and grow it.

Tony Robbins once said, "Don't go make a million dollars just for the money. Go make a million for the person you had to become to make the million." When you find the right network marketing business — should that be the route you choose to become an entrepreneur (it's the only business model that has personal growth built into it) — you will find that the personal development you'll gain is worth far more than the money you'll earn in the business. You will become more, and naturally you'll earn more.

But the lesson is to focus on you, on growing *you*. If you ever find your business hits a wall, it will mean you stopped working on *you*. Get back in there and sharpen your axe. Keep reading the right books, listen to the audios, attend the seminars, find the right mentors, and be coachable. At many points you will have to do a self-check to see if you've gotten ahead of yourself by letting your ego delude you into thinking you no longer need to surround yourself with big leaders who can keep you elevated and going even higher. When you're winning, keep winning. You'll know you're winning when you feel that self-respect as well as the respect of others around you.

FROM SUCCESS TO SIGNIFICANCE

Once I started to reach the pinnacle of success personally, and began living the life I had dreamed of, something dawned on me. I learned that success is all about me. Success is personal. It makes *my* life better, and affords *me* opportunities and luxuries.

When I began this journey at age 28, that's exactly what I wanted. I wanted to be wildly successful so I could have nice things, and so people would respect me. But then when I became successful by learning from great mentors, one of the things they taught me is how to be a mentor. I saw the joy they got from being an influence on my life. This is how I discovered this arc of progress from success to significance. Success is about you, but significance is about helping *others* have success — you become significant in other people's lives. This is the greatest feeling in the world. Making money is great, but being able to *give* money away to help others feels 10 times more fulfilling.

When I get emails or phone calls from people to tell me about how my involvement was instrumental in their success, and they express their gratitude for the time I gave them to help them win, that is when I feel like my life actually has significance. My life meant something to others. I made an impact. I made the world a better place.

This, my friend, is an amazing feeling. And it's a feeling that I hope one day you get to experience. It awaits you on the other end of this entrepreneurial journey. In the beginning, you put your own oxygen mask on first and focus on your personal success. But as that manifests in your life, it is my hope that you pay it forward and lift up as many others as possible and elevate their lives. I want you to live a life of significance.

COMMITMENT

The definition of commitment is doing what you said you would do long after the mood in which you said it has left you. Jim Rohn taught, "The same wind blows on us all. It's not the blowing of the wind but rather the setting of the sail that determines our destination." He also said, "Don't wish for things to get easier ... wish for *you* to get better."

What will you do when the going gets tough? Billionaire Mark Cuban spent 10 years working obsessively and barely getting by. But he stuck in there and now we all know what he's built.

As you go, you'll grow through some failures that you can

learn from. You'll feel growing pains. Naysayers will give you their unsolicited opinions. But your dogged determination to stick to your commitment and accomplish your WHY for starting your business in the first place is going to see you through to success.

You are going to make sacrifices for a season of your life — now — so that your future is better than ever. If you pick the right business, you won't have to work hard forever — only on the front end as you set things up. You know that at the counter of success, you have to pay full retail. There are no shortcuts or discounts. But you are willing to burn the candle at both ends for a season.

Because you are willing to do today what others won't do, you'll have tomorrow what others won't have. That's the payoff for the commitment and consistent efforts you will put forth. Your grandkids will be telling their kids how you built your empire and changed the family tree forever.

SHIFT HAPPENS

Making the shift is not easy. You have to make a decision and commit to it. When the going gets hard, you'll be tempted to fold up and go running back to the false sense of security of a job. But think about the company you work for. What if the founder of that company quit when turbulence came and he/she raced back to his/her job? Then the company you work for wouldn't exist today.

You will encounter trying times, and self-doubt will creep in. Just know that every single entrepreneur has encountered it, and the determined survived it. You just have to be so bought in that you will persevere through anything that comes your way. That's why mentors who've already weathered the storm are so invaluable.

Some new entrepreneurs don't treat their new enterprise as seriously as they treated their jobs. Maybe because they are under the ether of this newfound freedom to control their own schedule, they only work when they feel like it. Serious, successful entrepreneurs don't just work when they feel like it, they are *all in* and they work all the time during the building phase. They work when they're sick, when they're tired, on weekends, and on holidays. It's the price they're willing to pay up front to launch a business.

This is not a forever price — it's just on the front end. Time freedom will come down the road if you picked the right kind of business that has leverage and passive income. But you've got to go *all in* at the beginning to create it.

ACTION STEPS

Step 1 – Realize the need to become an entrepreneur. The time is now

Step 2 – Explore and decide on what business

Step 3 – Commit to the journey

Step 4 - Start a part-time business

Step 5 - Invest the earnings

Step 6 - Retire from your job and ramp up your efforts on your business

Step 7 - You're wealthy and free

Step 8 – Turn around and mentor others

You are about to experience something quite life-altering: For the first time in your life you will have an *end game*, an exit strategy. Knowing every day when you wake up that you're building something that will outlast you, that lives beyond your working days — *that*, my friend, is a feeling of exhilaration! I cannot feel it for you. I already know how it feels because I've lived with that exhilaration for over 20 years. You are going to feel a sense of mission and purpose like you've never felt. Commit to the journey, be a finisher and see what you start through to success.

So I just want to encourage you.

No time? *You've got to do this!*

No money? *You've got to do this!*

You don't think you can do this? *You've got to do this!*

Make the decision.

If you don't want to stay on the job path that will never get you to your dream lifestyle, you've got to make that decision *right now*.

At the end of the day, it all starts with a first step. Decide on a business and start part-time. You'll be surprised how quickly it can grow. You can either sell yourself on why you can't, or you'll sell yourself and why you *must*.

I hope that you make the decision today to go find the right business for you and get it rolling.

Change your life starting right now.

IN THEIR OWN WORDS

The danger of writing a book like this is that people may be tempted to believe that my advice is nothing more than ivory tower rhetoric. After all, I've had a lot of success as the result of my decision to start my own business and become an entrepreneur. It would be easy to believe that this kind of success doesn't really happen to ordinary, everyday people (as if I'm somehow extraordinary — I'm not).

For this reason, I've included the stories of a few others who exemplified courage and tenacity and saw entrepreneurialism as the vehicle to their dreams. Their stories span the spectrum of backgrounds — from ministry workers to mall managers, and from mortgage brokers to working moms. In many instances, the only thing that tied these folks together was their insatiable desire to break out of their going-nowhere careers — and get untrapped.

Their stories inspire me beyond words, and I know they will do the same for you

THE SUCCESS FORMULA
JORDAN A.

I think I was always a dreamer. As a young boy I always looked for ways to make extra money. I think this is the sign of a future entrepreneur. I would put on puppet and ventriloquist shows at the age of 7 and charge 25 cents for my friends to attend. I had a paper route in the neighborhood and it didn't matter if there was heavy snow or if it was a scorching hot day, I was up early to make sure the newspapers got delivered once a week. My objective was to figure out ways to get bigger tips from my customers because that's how I got paid.

I would handwrite thank you notes to each household and knock on doors in early December just to wish each family happy holidays. By being nice to my customers I would receive bigger tips than everyone else and that earned me bonuses and awards. I would shovel driveways and sidewalks in the winter and have lemonade stands in the summer. I was always in the lead when a contest was held for a fundraising drive because I was the one who made a list and asked the most people. I found myself to be very competitive and I always wanted to be recognized for winning. I noticed that some kids liked to be recognized for whining, which didn't get them very far.

A little later in life, I was introduced to the idea of residual income. I picked up a small book at a garage sale that introduced me to the idea of getting paid over and over again for working one time. I learned about vending machines, rental real estate, and network marketing. The idea of getting paid 24 hours a day sounded appealing. I had never even considered anything like this and it was never talked about in school! To me this idea represented a model for freedom in my life.

I had many business failures over the years. At the age of 23, I started a flight attendant training school. Competition popped up and put me out of business. I become an independent distributor for a number of companies that represented a vast array of products and services. I never could quite find the traction I needed to make any money.

At the age of 34, I was living in an enclosed garage. My job at the airline had cut my pay to $14,000 a year after filing for bankruptcy and I had run up my credit cards to $36,000. And then I became a distributor with a 3-year-old telecom network marketing company and, finally, all my preparation to be a real entrepreneur paid off. As cliché as it sounds, when preparation meets opportunity, everything changes.

Over the next 10 years, I earned in excess of $8 million. I moved out of that "garage" and into a beautiful A-frame home in the forest of Arizona. I purchased a couple of dream cars. I started traveling the world building my business, staying in the nicest hotels, and eating at the finest restaurants. And after 14 years, the market shifted drastically and we went from an exploding success story that experts were writing about to a sinking ship.

But I refused to quit because now I knew the success formula. I eventually busted out as the top distributor in a marketing company. I became a best-selling author of two books. I give more money away to charity per month than I used to make at my job in a year. I'm fulfilling two lifelong dreams of flying. Four years ago I attained a helicopter pilot's license and purchased my first helicopter. I'm also scheduled to become one of the first civilians in space with Richard Branson's Virgin Galactic Civilian Space Program.

I'm still learning and growing. Each year I strive to meet new people, fulfill new dreams and create new adventures. Flying to the stars is the metaphor I use to continue to soar in business and in life. I'm so grateful that I decided to take a risk and to become an entrepreneur. It's changed my life in ways I never could have dreamed possible.

BROKE NO MORE
DARNELL S.

I found myself working at a clothing store at a mall because I wanted to be able to buy designer clothes at a discount there. I planned to work there during college, but once I got my degree, I found that my tenure at the store was making me more money than I could earn by using my degree to get a new job. So I just stayed at the mall. You can probably imagine the life of a mall store manager. It was still dark in the mornings when I'd open the store, and it was dark when I'd close the store and head home.

Having one child while living this lifestyle was pretty difficult, but imagine adding a few additional kids into the mix! I missed out on so many personal events with the family because I ran these "stretch" shifts on weekends, and that's when most of life's special moments seemed to occur.

As a man, as a husband, and as a father, I'm sure you can empathize with how I was feeling. I knew that I had a ceiling at work I would never be able to break through. I felt like it was a dead end, but I couldn't afford to go elsewhere and start over. Beyond the money, I just wasn't being fulfilled. This is the kind of trap that you feel there is no way out of. I needed to get untrapped. I felt the internal push to do something bigger.

One day I answered an ad in the paper that said "MAR-KETING — If you keep doing what you're doing, nothing will change. Management skills helpful but not mandatory. Get paid while we train you!" I went and learned about a company that let you build your own business inside the company on a part-time basis, so I figured this might be my only way out. My eyes were opened to a whole new world of opportunity and potential, how to become an entrepreneur and escape the rat race.

I decided to go for it as an entrepreneur, but a few years in, it just wasn't happening. We fell three months behind on our mortgage and we had our car repossessed. I will never forget the bill collectors calling our home. The sense of despair or humiliation that each call brought to light may be hard to imagine if you've never lived it.

My first attempt at building my own business did not deliver the success I had hoped for, but I did learn so much about business and about myself. I discovered personal development and kept working on me. Then I met some mentors, and found myself surrounded by like-minded entrepreneurs. We created an accountability group and things began to blossom — my business finally got traction! In my first year with my new venture, I found myself earning more from my business from home than I used to make at the mall.

Within two years, my wife and I were not only stay-at-home parents for our four children, as we replaced both our salaries and no longer worked for anyone else, but we began living life by our design. We went on countless field trips and attended almost all of our kids' sporting events. We took our whole family on multiple trips, even internationally, every year. We helped so many other people discover entrepreneurial success that I was honored to be named Entrepreneur of the Year by the National Black Chamber of Commerce in 2004 and 2013. I founded a non-profit with my best friend that has adopted villages in Haiti and the Dominican Republic. We feed dozens of families in the D.C. area every Thanksgiving and Christmas, and we give away truckloads of toys in the area.

It is hard to put into print the indescribable feeling of being broke and without a car to now giving away cars. I am blessed beyond words to have this story. But I've learned that the greatest testimonies come as the result of having been tested. I don't regret the hard times because it made us realize we couldn't stay in that box, and we couldn't settle. The hard times were motivation and were our reason to pay the price to create a better life for our family. That is success. But significance is when you can proudly say you've helped hundreds of other families create success, and give their kids back their parents.

Had my eyes never been opened to a better way, who knows where we'd be right now. It's my mission to keep sharing our story so more people can create better lives for themselves, too.

SAILING TO SUCCESS
GERRY & SALLIE H.

The Best Product Any Business Can Offer is . . . LIFESTYLE!

Before discovering network marketing, my wife, Sallie, and I had successful but separate careers, me as a real estate investor and she in corporate America. For me, buying and selling more than 30 real estate properties in California proved to be extremely profitable but when the economy turned bad, or when tax laws changed, or when interest rates soared to 21%, I realized that because I couldn't control those external factors, it was time to start looking for a business model where I had greater control over my financial success.

Sallie, on the other hand, made a six-figure income in her corporate position but she didn't have the time to enjoy her success. She was working 60 hours a week, traveling all over the country, and missing the best moments of her two daughters' lives. She wanted to find a way to replace her income without having to work so hard and still have more time to enjoy the family she loved.

Starting a home-based business provided the solution we were both looking for. Not only did we have more free time to enjoy our success, but when the economy turned bad — which it often does — it actually brought more business partners to our team, thereby increasing our success.

When Gerry met Sallie (sounds like a familiar movie, right?) I was actually living on my sailboat. We quickly fell in love and I promised Sallie that her life with me would never be dull. We bareboat chartered a beautiful sailing ketch in Greece for our honeymoon, and sailed by ourselves to 17 incredible Greek islands. We had so many amazing adventures that we made the decision to pick a new exotic location every year and spend a month or more sailing wherever the wind chose to blow.

Over the years, we've cruised on month-long charters in locales like the south coast of France and Italy, the British, U.S., and Spanish Virgin Islands (twice!), the Sea of Cortez, the Leeward Islands of the Caribbean, the Hawaiian Islands, the Windward Islands of the Caribbean, and the southwest coast of Turkey (twice!). Our next sailing adventure will take us to Croatia for a full month where we've bareboat chartered a 42-foot sloop (a sailing boat with a single mast)!

But spending one month out of the year on the water wasn't enough! It had always been our dream to return to living full-time on the water and our network marketing business has made that dream a reality. Thanks to the powerful network marketing business model, our dream came true when we purchased (for all cash!) a three-story, 70-foot motor yacht, Slice of Life, and now get to live on the water! And when we're not living on our own boat or bareboat cruising on chartered sailboats, we also enjoy cruising the world on big cruise ships.

In early 2018, we took a 28-day cruise to Tahiti. In 2019, we sailed from Los Angeles to Hawaii and then on to Alaska for another 27 days. Our next big cruise will take us on a full 60-day journey around the entire Pacific Rim, back up to Alaska, and then over to Asia and the South Pacific.

What we love most about our yacht-based "home" business is that we have no employees to deal with, no store to run, no inventory to worry about, and none of the other hassles associated with owning a traditional business. This gives us the freedom to travel whenever we want and enjoy life even though we have a large and rapidly growing business.

Our daily deposits include renewal income that's based on monthly membership premiums. We get paid over and over again, not just on the memberships we've sold but also on all the memberships sold by our entire team. That's what allows them us live our dream lifestyle. I know lots of people who make six figures like we do, but I like the way we make ours 10 times more.

Instead of going off in separate directions to a job every day, we get to work side-by-side together building our dreams while supporting others to reach their dreams as well. Who could ask for a better purpose in life?

CRUSHING CURVEBALLS
KAREN L.

I was working in corporate America as an executive administrative assistant. I did not have a college education, but the job was decent so I tolerated it. Deep inside, though, I was miserable because my dream was to be a stay-at-home mom. Dropping my kids off at daycare, peeling them off of me, and leaving them all day was brutal.

My father, who always had my best interest in mind, introduced me to an opportunity to start my own business from home. I decided to give it a shot because it just made sense. I didn't exactly set the world on fire at first, but in short order it did allow me to make my dream came true to be a stay-at-home mom. When I did my very first presentation, I made more that day than I made in a month working a 40-hour week!

My mentor pushed me a lot because she knew where I was at that time of my life. With a full plate at home, she encouraged me to just turn it on high, which is what I did. I worked hard at building my business. During that time, I met my future husband, Paul, who was also working in the same home-based business. We got married in 2006 and worked our businesses together. Within our first two years of marriage, our residual income kicked in, which really supercharged our household income. We used the opportunity that leveraged income afforded us and traveled and just loved our life.

But sometimes life throws you a curveball or two — or three. I was diagnosed with Stage 2 lung cancer. I went through all the necessary scans and was told that they were going to do surgery and if the cancer had spread, they were going to remove the mass in my lung and begin chemo. But if it had not spread, they were simply going to remove the mass. On the day of the procedure, they removed a third of my lung, but I was told that it was not cancer! Instead, it was a massive blood clot that had gone through my heart and had killed off a big portion of my lung. Tragedy avoided, right? Not exactly. Another curveball was headed right toward us.

A few months after my surgery, Paul started complaining of pain in his side. He was told it was probably a gallbladder infection, so we ended up going to the emergency room at 5:30 in the morning where they found lesions on his liver. A CT scan revealed he that he had Stage 4 pancreatic cancer. We had to travel to Illinois every other week for treatment. Between the ravages of the disease and the rigors of travel, it got to be too much, so we decided to complete the treatments back home at Ohio State University. Fourteen months later, Paul was gone.

Curveball number three arrived only two months after Paul died; I was diagnosed with colon cancer. I had to have part of my colon removed during a period of time when I hadn't even fully grieved the loss of my husband.

While the losses were devastating, there was definitely a silver lining: While we were going through Paul's ordeal, and then later my own, our home-based business ensured deposits in our bank account every single day. We never had to worry about paying our bills, paying for our kids, or anything else. We didn't have to take time off of work or worry about "sick days" or using vacation time. We just focused entirely on fighting for each other's lives. We never missed a single scan, blood draw, or hospital appointment. More importantly, we didn't miss a single minute of each other's time — and our income just kept on growing.

I often think if I were in my corporate America job, I would have lost it during that time. During the 14 months of Paul's ordeal, between chemo, follow-up appointments, palliative care, etc., we were in and out of a hospital almost every single day. After my own cancer challenge, I had days when I had a hard time getting on my feet, and there were times when I couldn't work or do anything else. But the beauty of having my own home-based business was that I could pick and choose when I was strong enough to work.

My mantra in life is: Make a memory, because life is so short. I still live in the same house as when we were making $50,000 a year. But now I earn more than $300,000. Because I'm able to call the shots, I'm spending more and more time building and maintaining relationships and focusing on things that really matter, and not worrying about how to divide my time between my corporate job and the people I cherish the most.

ENTREPRENEUR FOR LIFE
PATRICK M.

Later in life, I graduated college and knew right away that I wanted to start a business. The challenge I had — that most people have — is the high cost of starting a business. I didn't have the tens of thousands of dollars that are usually needed to get something like that off the ground. So I was the guy who was washing cars, cutting people's grass, selling t-shirts — doing things to create revenue and be a business owner. These were businesses that I could basically run off a credit card. But I didn't have a franchise-type of business, per se. I just knew that I didn't want to be stuck in a job, and that's why I was so willing to try some of these endeavors.

I was introduced to a company that employed the network marketing model. I saw that they had a proven system, that I could get quality mentorship, and that I could potentially make a significant income without having to put out a lot of big money out-of-pocket. It just made sense, so I did this part-time for the first year and then went full-time the second year. It turned out to be the very best thing I've ever done because I've made millions in the past 15 years.

Needless to say, taking the bold step and starting my own business in this framework has changed my life in all the ways you'd expect millions of dollars to change your life! But beyond that, it's given me choices; it's given me time freedom; it's given the opportunity to do what I want and to help the people I love. It's given me the ability to reach back and help other people as well. In our industry you'll usually find that the people who are very successful really love other people. Once you make money, there are a lot of other things you can do with your money to make even more money. This business is really for those who love people and love helping people win.

I also love personal development —it's one of the "requirements" to success when you start your own business. So, you're definitely going to continue to grow. This is a culture that fosters growth and allows you to circulate in a world that is fertilized with personal development.

My business also allowed me to go around the world and help lots of people. My nanny, for instance, is from Colombia. I brought her into my organization and I helped her make thousands her first month! She was an immigrant who had been a nanny for a professional baseball player, and when they were done raising their three children, they packed her stuff, put her out in the front yard, and said, "Thanks for your service." But when she's done raising my kids, she's going to have financial dignity. I helped her sign up 3,000 customers in Columbia that she's going to generate money from. That's the power of a home-based business, and that's the power of helping other people!

Back to my dad. He was the ultimate company guy. He was the "I'll-do-whatever-you-need-me-to do" guy. He never said no to anything he was asked to do at work. But after

30 years, they just didn't need him anymore. Unfortunately, that's not uncommon. The corporate world is not designed to take care of people; that's our job.

Being a self-employed person is not always easy because you don't have a track to learn alone and you don't usually have mentors, but if you find the right opportunity and you plug into a system that already been developed, has already been proven, and has consistently yielded positive results, the journey will change your life. And I am living proof.

LOVING MONDAYS
PAUL B.

Most people hate going to work on Mondays. Not me. I loved my job. I couldn't wait to get to work on Monday. I was working my dream job in ministry. It provided me with a sense of purpose, passion, and direction. I got to travel the world (on someone else's dime!), meet incredible people, and make a difference on a huge scale. I was happy to exchange my time (between 50-60 hours a week) for money because I loved my job. There was only one problem: I was never able to get ahead.

On my job, we would get paid on the 15th and the 30th of each month. When I got paid on the 15th, I would pay all my bills and I was flat broke on the 16th. So I would white-knuckle it until the end of the month, get paid on the 30th, pay my bills, and I was flat broke on the next day. There was literally nothing left over. There was no way to put money aside, build wealth, or even have an emergency fund. It was a dangerous way to live, but I was quick to overlook it because of how much I enjoyed my job.

The turning point came for me when my wife announced she was pregnant with our first child. Simple economics told me that if we were just barely getting by now, there was no way we were going to be able to skate by with a child in tow! I went into panic mode and reviewed my options. I could try to get a second job, but how was that going to work if I was already putting in 50+ hours a week? When exactly was I supposed to work the second job? The other option was to have my wife get a second job, but she was about to give birth to our child — was this really the best time for her to be starting a second job? This was a problem.

It became very apparent to me that the best way to solve this quandary was to look into a home-based opportunity. I'd heard of these for years but never really looked into them. I spent the next several months looking at every home-based business under the sun! I was very particular about the kind of business I would consider, and I spent a considerable amount of time thoroughly investigating the companies that I considered to be contenders. As my search came to a close, I was discouraged because I couldn't find anything that matched the criteria I required. So I gave up. I stopped searching. I went back to the grind.

But once the mind expands, it can never go back. During my months of search, I had also entered into a season of intense personal development. I was starting to become the person I wanted to be. My mind started to expand. I saw opportunities I had never noticed before. So when a business magazine fell into my lap that highlighted a network marketing company that had created more than 200 millionaires and thousands of others who were earning extraordinary incomes, I had already been primed to be receptive to the information.

I liked what I saw about this company and decided to dip my toes into the water to see if they could help me generate an extra $500 a month from home. Within a very short period of time, I was not only making that, but was able to pay the full mortgage on my house without ever having to touch my regular income. The best part was, I was only putting in around five hours a week! Still, though, I wasn't looking for a career change or life change. I was content to leave things the way they were. But then everything changed.

On a sunny Monday morning, my boss called me into his office and told me the job I loved so much was going away. I was crushed — but not defeated. I knew that if I could pay the mortgage on my house putting in only a few hours a week, I could certainly make much more if I put in a few more hours. Fast forward: Within four months of the day I got laid off, I was able to match the monthly income that it took me 14 years to build!

Today life is very, very different. I haven't worked a job now in 10 years. I don't intend to ever work one again! I'm making more money than I ever have in my life, but more importantly, I've got my time back. I attend all of my son's activities, I pick him up from school every day, my family goes on trips and vacations for as long as we want ... and I never have to ask for anyone's permission, use up "vacation days," or try to get creative with "sick days."

Starting a home-based business is the best thing I've ever done, and daring to leave the comfort of the semi-monthly paycheck for the exhilaration of building my own empire has been a game-changer beyond my wildest dreams.

RECLAIMING MOTHERHOOD
SUSAN MARIE A.

I was definitely influenced to follow in my father's footsteps as I was growing up. I watched Dad go off to the office each day, heard him having important conversations with clients, and on rare occasions got to visit him at work. He was an attorney, and I indeed followed that lead! I went to law school, and practiced law for 12 years. When I started having children, however, my priorities changed.

I did not want to be cooped up in an office while someone else raised my daughters. It was right about that time that my friend, who was the librarian at the school where I was teaching criminal justice part time, took me to lunch and introduced network marketing to me. She was nervous to show me the information, especially when I asked her point-blank if it was network marketing, but she braved through it, and I was intrigued originally because I saw it as a potential "referral source."

I definitely had no intention of working the business full time; I simply thought it would be a good supplement to my teaching income. Not in a million years I did not foresee the day (which came shortly thereafter) where it would become the primary source for the household that it eventually became! Within the first year, I hit the highest level in my company's compensation structure and became a six-figure earner shortly thereafter.

I plugged in to the system of training and events and before I knew it, I was receiving an education about becoming an entrepreneur that matched any degree I could have gotten from a formal school! I've been exposed to the concepts of leveraged and residual income, entrepreneurship, and leadership.

This industry continues to positively impact my life and support me in becoming a better person because I am in business for myself, while at the same time moving forward with an ever-expanding team of amazing individuals. We learn and grow together, as new horizons present themselves and are attained.

My two daughters, who were toddlers when I started, are the greatest recipients of the rewards of those new levels of growth. Being self-employed allowed me to work my business around my daughters' lives. Yes, they saw the sacrifice that hard work requires (such as time in my home office on the phone, one evening a week at a business briefing, and one Saturday a month at an event), but they also saw the beautiful reward of flexibility that allowed for my presence and involvement with them.

Now, nearly 2 decades down the road, my daughters are young adults themselves and are in my business alongside me, while they pursue their college degrees! The freedom I had to be with my daughters while they grew up, and the ability to send them to a private school along the way, were invaluable treasures. Nevertheless, a treasure beyond that has been the positive impact of them being raised inside a community where goals are set and actively pursued!

My children saw me work, but they also never saw me work outside the home at a 9-to-5 job. Instead, they saw me working towards earning incentive trips, for example, and have often said that's been one of their favorite parts of my being in network marketing!

Today, because of the choice my husband and I made to go full-time with network marketing, we also get to help other families realize their goals and to believe in the power of their dreams! That kind of reward is so profound I can confidently say that ours is a family that is in network marketing for life, and I'll be eternally grateful to the gal who introduced me to it!

NO MORE GROUNDHOG DAY
TARA W.

I was working full-time in a wholesale mortgage business. I sold loans to the people who sold loans to people. I worked a little bit from home in the morning and then I had to go on my field calls, visit my brokers, etc.

I had a 1-year-old and a 7-year-old and my husband had a full-time job. Even though we lived in Northern California where the cost of living is ridiculously high, we both had six-figure incomes so we were doing fine. We didn't have a lot of debt; we just lived comfortably in a tiny 1,200 square-foot condo.

We were relatively happy but every single day was like Groundhog Day — it was exactly the same: Get up to an alarm clock, grab some coffee, wake the kids and get them dressed, pack their lunches, ship off one to school and the other to daycare, work all day long, pick the kids up between 5:00 and 5:30, go home, cook dinner, clean dishes, do some homework, get them to bed, and collapse on the couch. Every day. Every. Single. Day.

I always wondered what if I started my own mortgage company, or what if we started our own business or franchise? But I didn't have enough any money saved up and I didn't have any good ideas. When I was first approached regarding network marketing, my first thought was how in the world would I be able to put something else on my plate? I felt like I didn't have any disposable time. I didn't want to spend more time away from my children for just a little bit of extra money. I would have given away half my salary to be home with my children. I was already making good money, but now there was an opportunity to make even more money and have control of my own time to be with my kids.

So I committed to learning — and I failed miserably for a few months! But I attended a big event where I saw the larger vision and six months after coming out of that event, I replaced my six-figure income. Twelve months after that event, I tripled my six-figure income. It's now been 12 years and I've earned more than $5 million … and I'm still going! Two years into having my new career, I had my third child. The feeling of not having to look at that looming date on the calendar when I have to go back to work, like I did with my first child, was a feeling that I want every mother to feel, and to be able to say to her child, "I don't have to go back to work and leave you all day."

We've been able to replace my husband's income tenfold. I started making in one month what my husband was making all year, so we decided it was probably time for him to come home, too! Today, my kids have two full-time parents. We work from home, we trade off dropping off and picking up the kids, and we're heavily involved in their sports. That's been invaluable to me. So has the ability to take a three-week vacation and not have to ask anybody.

If it wasn't for a close family member strongly encouraging me to look at this, I probably wouldn't have. My advice to everyone is to always be open-minded. I absolutely believe that everyone has 20 to 25 hours a week that they can devote to building their dream — even if they have a full-time job. I can prove it. It's all about making the time. If you really, really want this you'll make the time.

This industry has given me a life I would never, ever have had. What an amazing feeling knowing that my "backup plan" became my legacy.

EPILOGUE

If you're waiting for your all your ducks to be lined up in a row before you get started in a business, it'll never happen because your ducks are never going to be in a row. As a matter fact, your ducks are dog tired and have stopped trying to line up with you. Waiting for the perfect time is a fool's game. There will never be a perfect time in the future. There will always be something that you will pin your procrastination on. The perfect time is *right now*, even though it may not seem like it.

Let's go back to the future ...

It's five years from now, and it's 10:15 a.m. on a Tuesday. Are you sitting in an office wishing for a better life? Or are you peering out the window of your dream home — or out the window of a plane heading on another vacation visiting far-off countries?

If you keep doing what you're doing, you'll keep getting what you're getting. If better is possible, it's your duty to go get it.

Five years from now, what would you go back and tell yourself today? Would you urgently advise yourself to not waste another minute and make the shift to change your life now?

There's no such thing as a fearless leader, only a courageous one. Same thing with entrepreneurs. You can't wait until the fear of taking action goes away, because it won't.

I'm pulling for you that you'll make that *courageous* choice today!

THE END

... or THE BEGINNING (you decide)

I hope you'll pass this book on and change someone else's life.

For bulk pricing to get more copies to share, go to UntrappedBook.com.

For additional coaching on how to become an entrepreneur, and to see videos from the author, go to UntrappedBook.com.

APPENDIX

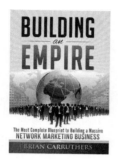

Anyone looking to succeed in building a business should read my book, **Building an Empire – The Most Complete Blueprint to Building a Massive Network Marketing Business**. *www.BuildingAnEmpireBook.com*

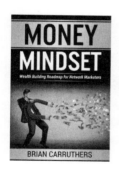

After your business has begun flowing cash your way, you will want to learn how to pay the least amount of taxes by leveraging all the write-offs available to entrepreneurs, how to keep as much as you can and invest it effectively so that your money is growing while you are sleeping. Read this book, *www.moneymindsetbook.com.*

Empire Builders Pro is the #1 mobile platform for building a direct selling business, with coaching and tools from Brian Carruthers — discover it at *EmpireBuildersPro.com.*

ABOUT THE AUTHOR

BRIAN CARRUTHERS

B rian became an entrepreneur at an early age. He always knew that he wanted to build his own empire — not that he knew just how he was going to do it. Growing up, he worked jobs in the summers, but all year round he had some sort of business going. At age 12, Brian cut eight lawns a week to earn money to invest in his baseball card collection, which he turned into a business. He washed cars on weekends, caught crabs and sold them door to door, sold newspapers, chopped wood to sell as firewood, and even convinced his mom to help him cook French fries that he could walk down the beach selling to sunbathers.

When Brian returned home to Maryland from getting his accounting degree from Villanova University, he knew he was never planning to be an accountant. Sure, he'd hire accountants one day, but he wanted more wealth and freedom than that could provide. He began his career in the family real estate business. Brian was rookie of the year for his

county at age 21, and went on to enjoy a successful career selling homes. But along the way, his vision was widened by his associations with some extremely successful entrepreneurs who showed him a world where he could have it all — wealth and time freedom together. Brian made a decision to pursue a home-based business that elicited laughter from some folks at first, but later caused those same people to call him a "genius." Why would someone already making six figures and who was in line to step into ownership one day of a 24-office real estate company see the need to do anything else? While others didn't quite understand this decision, Brian knew he was onto something big. He knew he was not only going to build serious wealth, but he was going to help countless people find their freedom and get untrapped themselves.

To date, Brian has spoken on stages at entrepreneurial events with the likes of Sir Richard Branson, Paul J. Meyer, Tony Robbins, Grant Cardone, Pitbull, Robert Kiyosaki, Eric Worre, Charlie Tremendous Jones, John C. Maxwell, Harvey Mackay, Daymond John, and many others. Brian's first three books became immediate best sellers in their category. He has hundreds of thousands of followers all around the world, and his name is heard in the testimonies of many successful entrepreneurs quite often.

Brian works from his home office in Virginia with his family. He enjoys travel, golfing, fishing, and hunting for fossil shark's teeth. Aside from his family, the topmost thing on his mind every single day is how can he help more people discover the vehicle to build their wealth and gain their freedom. This is Brian's calling and his mission.